MARLEY

MARLEY

1945 – 1981

BARRY LAZELL

HAMLYN

CONTENTS

Picture Acknowledgements

Archive Photos: 23, 60
Andes Press Agency: Carlos Reyes 22 top, 80 top left
Aquarius Picture Library: 25 top
Camera Press: 8 top, Colin Jones 46 bottom, Lennox Smillie 46 centre, 66 centre, 74, 76 bottom
Colorific: Annie Leibovitz /Contact 2, 33, 35 left
Hulton Deutsch Collection: 8 centre, 9, 10 left, 21 bottom, 30, 32 bottom
Impact Photos: Alain le Garsmeur 13 top, 16, Colin Jones 7 top, 11, 14 bottom, 17, 26, Piers Cavendish 62
London Features International: 18 left, 18 right, 35 centre, 38 bottom, 73, 79 bottom, Michael Putland 1, 42 centre, 52, Michael Ochs 15, Ann Summa 67 bottom, Angie Coqueran 72 bottom, Jill Furmanovsky 57 left and right
Magnum: Alex Webb 45 bottom, H.Gruyaert 66 bottom, Rene Burri 76 top
Pictorial Press: 4–5, 10 right, 19 bottom, 21 top, 37, Bob Gruen /Starfile 65 top, Chuck Pulin /Starfile 71
Barry Plummer: 41 bottom, 64
Popperfoto: 18 centre
Redferns: 45 top, Gems 8 bottom, William Gottlieb 10 centre, Erica Echenberg 31 bottom, David Redfern 35 right, 40, 49, Ian Dickson 36, 39, Ebet Roberts 47, 58 bottom, 77, G. Wiltshire 48, A. Putler 61 centre, M. Prior 61 right
Relay Photos Ltd: A. Byrne 32 centre, Chris Walter 63 top
Repfoto: 44, 63 bottom,:Robert Ellis 31 top, 53 top, 80 bottom left
Retna: 42 bottom, Steve Rapport 12, David Corio 53 bottom, 79 top, Paul Slattery 55, 80 right, Ari Diesendruck 72 top
Rex Features: 19, 22 bottom, 29, 34, 41 top, 65 bottom, 75, SIPA-Press 14 top, 22 centre, 66 top, 69 bottom, 69 top, Chris Brown /SIPA-Press 50, 51, Lafaille /SIPA-Press 70, Lynn Goldsmith 32 top, Linda Matlock /Pix 67 top, Lance Lummsden 68
Frank Spooner Pictures: GAMMA 38 top, 54 centre, Serge Assier /GAMMA 54 top, Laine /Ricards /Liaison 78
Sygma: Jacques Pavlovsky 61 left, Patrick Chauvel 42 top, 43, 46 top, 54 bottom, 58 top, 59
Topham: 7 bottom, 13 bottom, 24, 56

Editor: **Mike Evans**
Production Controller: **Michelle Thomas**
Picture Research: **Liz Fowler**
Art Editor: **Ashley Western**
Design: **Margaret Sadler**

First published in 1994 by
Hamlyn, an imprint of
Reed Consumer Books Limited,
Michelin House, 81 Fulham Road,
London SW3 6RB
and Auckland, Melbourne, Singapore and Toronto

Copyright © 1994 Reed International Books Limited

A Catalogue record for this book is available from the British Library
ISBN 0–600–58221–3

Printed and bound in Spain by Cayfosa, Barcelona.

ROOTS

Robert Nesta Marley was born at 2:30am on Tuesday, February 6, 1945, in the village of Nine Miles in the mountainous rural parish of St. Ann, northern Jamaica. The six-and-a-half-pound baby, as even his coffee-coloured new-born appearance made clear, was the product of a mixed-race marriage. His mother was a young, unsophisticated black woman, the 19-year-old Cedella (known universally as Ciddy) Marley, a daughter of farmer Omeriah Malcolm, Nine Miles' unofficial head citizen. The child's father was Captain Norval Sinclair Marley, a diminutive, softly-spoken white man more than 30 years his wife's senior, and one of two sons of a middle-class Jamaican family with English antecedents, originally from the parish of Clarendon.

His military title came from his time with the British West Indian Regiment, in which he had been a quartermaster but, when he first met 17-year-old Cedella in 1943, he was an overseer of the northern Crown Lands on the island, a mobile occupation which involved frequent short stays in the various rural parishes and settlements. On one such spell in the Nine Miles district, an attraction – and, before long, a passionate romance – developed between the ostensibly ill-matched Norval and Cedella, a liaison which was frowned upon by the extended Malcolm clan who populated much of the locality.

When Cedella found, in May 1944, that she was pregnant, Norval Marley, to her family's considerable surprise and not inconsiderable concern, pledged to marry her and to support the child. A rapidly convened wedding took place on the second Friday in June and then, on the very next day, Captain Marley departed on horseback to Kingston, effectively riding out of his young wife's life. She only ever saw him again during brief and infrequent visits.

Jamaica's social conditions and political makeup in the middle of the 20th century were the legacy of centuries of British colonial rule, and of the comparatively recent roots of much of the population in slavery.

Top: Marcus Garvey, the labour organiser, orator and somewhat ostentatious visionary and founder of the United Negro Improvement Association
Centre: A typical village church, Lacocia, Jamaica
Bottom: Marley's mother, Cedella Booker
Opposite: Emperor Haille Selassie I, seated in state in Addis Ababa

Until slave emancipation in 1834, Jamaica had been run, essentially, as a huge sugar plantation, the product and profits of which went to colonial masters overseas. Its majority black population had been forcibly imported from Africa in the 17th century as slave labour for this enterprise. When Robert Nesta was born, over a century after emancipation, the material lot of many of the descendents of those slaves had barely improved, with poverty still endemic and social advancement an empty hope for most black Jamaicans. In Kingston, the capital city, the ghettoisation of the have-nots from the haves, the blacks from the whites, was starkly evident in the shanty towns where hunger and overcrowding were the norm, crime a near-inevitability, religion the only source of hope, and music and dance the only comfort.

An impotent bitterness at the lot of the average black Jamaican simmered constantly below the surface of everyday shanty town life, frequently expressed in the form of self-destructive violence. The most coherent expression of black disaffection in Jamaica had come in the early 1900s from another St. Ann native, Marcus Garvey. He was a labour organiser, orator and somewhat entrepreneurial visionary, who preached the gospel of a mass exodus of black people from the Caribbean and the Americas to Africa, where Garvey foretold the establishment of a black state free of colonialism and the white man. His organisation, the United Negro Improvement Association, was formed to put these ideas into practice, and he even founded a shipping company, the Black Star Line (in which only blacks could invest), as a first step towards providing the means of such repatriation, but despite early enthusiasm – particularly when he took his ideas and oratory to the USA – his efforts eventually foundered on the rocks of hostile authority, and he was to die in England in 1940 with none of his aims brought to fruition. However, he did leave behind him in Jamaica one important, if initially intangible legacy – his rallying cry which spoke of Africa as the spiritual black homeland. Its assimilation into the collective black Jamaican consciousness was undoubtedly a factor in the establishment of Rastafarianism in Jamaica in the 1930s, even though Garvey himself would have no truck with the new religion during his lifetime. Many of his acolytes, however, along with the followers of several existing Afrocentrist semi-religious cults, believed that something of great import was signified by the coronation, in 1930, of a new Emperor of Ethiopia.

Ras Tafari Makkonen, an Ethiopian prince, claimed direct lineage from King Solomon. At the age of 38, after some years steering a course through the medieval world of Ethiopian royal power politics, he was crowned Emperor as Haile Selassie I, fulfilling both the Afro-centrist prophesies of a black African Messiah who would lead his people back to the motherland, and the Garveyist dream of a symbolic black African

monarch who would be of significance on the world stage. For both groups, Selassie represented the hope of negro deliverance, but as World War II engulfed much of the globe there was no sign of this hope being realised in any secular sense; instead, it was as a spiritual figure that his stature in Jamaica subsequently grew. Rastafarians (the word was a straightforward adaptation of Selassie's given name) found a refuge from the world of the oppressor by, essentially, losing interest in it and focusing on the spiritual horizon instead. Bob Marley and the immediate world around him were untouched by the faith while he was

launched big island hits by home-grown talents like Lord Kitchener and the Mighty Sparrow.

A gradual influx of American jump blues and R&B during the 1950s, mostly relayed from black radio stations in Miami as transistor radios slowly infiltrated Jamaica, mutated mento and calypso into ska. This was a form wholly developed on Jamaican soil by local musicians, attempting to perform their own covers of the music coming from the US, like Louis Jordan's and Wynonie Harris's danceable jump blues or Fats Domino's New Orleans R&B.

growing up; it would be in his young adult life that, in search of wider visions than the deprived world of the Kingston slums, Marley would match his impatient (almost Garveyite) visionary stance with the calmer homeward-looking spiritual pride of the Rastafari.

Robert Nesta lived alongside music throughout his early life, most of it overtly spiritual, since his mother Ceddy was a devout churchgoer. In Jamaica, as in most former slave territories, both religious and secular native music tended to combine elements, mostly rhythmic, which had been retained through many generations from transported African origins, with a leavening of European influence appropriated from the colonial masters.

A wholly West Indian, if not Jamaican, form of popular music had arisen between the two world wars in the shape of calypso, a folky, lighthearted and frequently comedy-orientated genre which could be adapted easily to almost any topical lyrical requirements. It became identifiable worldwide as the 'sound' of the Caribbean, and by the 1940s its renewable topicality had been combined with the locally-developed dance-rhythmic mento style to create a commercial hybrid which

Left: A traditional West Indian calypso singer
Centre: Louis Jordan with his Tympani Five
Right: The Drifters in 1956 with (l to r) Jimmy Oliver, Gerhart Thrasher, Johnny Moore, Charlie Hughes and pianist Tommy Evans

It is doubtful that young Marley was exposed to any of this music in the rural (and transistor-less) environs of St. Ann. When he and his mother eventually settled in Kingston, however, ska music would be ever-present as an integral part of the sound of the city, inextricably bound with the harsh realities of ghetto life. It would be only a matter of time before ska, in turn, would be hearing from Bob Marley.

In 1959, when Nesta Marley was 14, Ciddy's brother Solomon, who had a room in a Trench Town government yard (the Kingstonian equivalent of low-rental, low-amenity coucil housing) at 19 Second Street, announced that he intended to emigrate to England, and would let Ciddy take it over after he had left. This slum yard was to be Bob Marley's home for the impressionable years of his late childhood and

young adolescence, and it was there he found a soulmate in another, slightly younger, immigrant from the country, whose name was Neville Livingston, though universally known as Bunny. He was the son of Thadeus (Toddy) Livingston, a friend of Ciddy's who was their immediate neighbour in the yard and shared their kitchen. Although the boys did not attend school together (Nesta went to the fee-paying Model Private School, which ate up virtually all Ciddy's spare resources), they were otherwise inseparable. They shared a passion for soccer, kicking a tattered but prized football around the yard and alleyways for hours at a time, until darkness (there was no electric street lighting in Trench Town) forced a halt. Both also loved to sing, and developed a passion for the American music they heard for the first time via a transistor radio owned by one of their yard neighbours, always turned up loud and tuned at night to an R&B station from Miami or New Orleans. Familiarity would soon have them singing along to US group hits like the Drifters' There Goes My Baby and the Moonglows' Ten Commandments Of Love, and R&B ballads like Sam Cooke's Wonderful World and Brook Benton's So Many Ways .

The Rastaman, with his red, gold and green livery, was becoming a common sight as Bob Marley grew up in Jamaica

During his final two school years, Robert Nesta ceased to pay much further attention to formal learning. Instead, his education was coming from his environment, from his ghetto peers and from the general 'runnings' of the street culture in Trench Town. In order to survive, a teenage boy had to learn the arts of the street: to defend himself in a fist fight – with a knife when necessary – and to spar verbally with others in the vernacular of the 'rude boys', the hooligan element whose delinquency was a fact of West Kingston life. Nesta, who had always been something of an observer and a little apart from the crowd, nevertheless found himself drawn to the on-edge cameraderie which existed here. If his small stature (around five feet) made him theoretically vulnerable, his quick wits and the intimidating aura he could project – centred around his silent, dark, penetrating gaze – brought him street respect aplenty.

However, he and Bunny were not bent on becoming rude boys, but singers and musicians. Bunny had thrown himself together a home-made guitar, literally from available scrap (a king-size sardine can played a major part), and the duo were constantly refining their repertoire of radio-taught R&B and doo-wop, plus the new sound system style known as ska.

The duo could hear the ska hits by hanging around after school near Coxsone's Musik City, a record shop set up by producer and veteran sound system organiser Clement Dodd, known to the masses as 'Sir Coxsone'. Dodd and his close rival Duke Reid had been Jamaica's mobile dance kings since the mid-1950s, and the scene's most judicious users of hot, closely-guarded US hit singles as money-making audience rousers. When American R&B began to mellow out around 1960, both men moved in to fill the void with their own hot, dance-friendly material custom-performed and produced in Jamaica. R&B-based but with native lacings of mento and calypso, it settled quickly into a recognisable rhythm form identifiable by a universal name – ska. Once ska singles by local artists like Laurel Aitken, Jackie Edwards, Owen Gray and Derrick Morgan became hot at the island's dances, they could and did become successful with the wider Jamaican public on disc. An indigenous record industry, strictly cottage-sized and with notoriously chaotic business practices, sprang up at the dawn of the 1960s, and the sound system entrepreneurs were in its vanguard, operating their own studios, labels, shops and pressing plants. Coxsone's Musik City was the street outlet of one such operation, and Nesta and Bunny were fascinated by it. As they learned and emulated the sounds which Sir Coxsone blasted out into the street from his record shop, they also became aware after a while that if they were to take their own music any further than harmonising it in the yard, the means of doing so, and the people who could help them, were fortuitously close at hand.

When his school days ended in the summer of 1961, Nesta announced to Ciddy that he was going to become a musician. However, she, abetted by Toddy Livingston, had different ideas regarding his future welfare. When he left the classroom, 'Bob' Marley – as his rude boy acquaintances now called him (he requested his family to do like-wise, since it had the 'ring' of his more adult status) – headed not for the recording studio, but for a local workshop where Toddy had got him apprenticed as a welder.

Record shops in Jamaica, like the one below in Montego Bay, were often ramshackle affairs similar to the shanty towns they occupied

EARLY WAILERS

Cedella Marley was aware that her son would hate the job she and Toddy had found for him at a local welder's, though she knew that – for all his running around with, and growing reputation for toughness among the local 'rudies' – Bob would accept it out of duty to her. So he did, while inwardly vowing that it would only be temporary while he got his musical ambitions underway. The drudgery of repairing bike frames spurred him into practical career moves.

For advice and practical tuition, he sought out Joe Higgs, resident in a neighbouring yard, and something of a Jamaican musical hero. As Higgs & Wilson, the Rastafarian singer-songwriter and his regular harmony partner Roy Wilson had had a major Jamaican hit single in 1959

with Higgs' self-penned Manny-O, and the duo were still a major attraction around Kingston. Bob realised that he could learn vital things about songs, singing and performance from his neighbour, and Higgs was happy to impart his wisdom. In fact, he held an almost daily informal music school in his yard, tutoring local would-be vocalists via his own extensive practical and theoretical knowledge, plus a repertoire of songs in styles from calypso to R&B and jazz. Bob and Bunny became regulars at these Third Street sessions, and while many others came fascinated then drifted away disillusioned – because Higgs, for all his sharing generosity, was an exacting tutor and a harsh critic of lazy performance – they stuck at it, learning to sing not only together but in close harmony, Bunny's near-falsetto blending strongly with Bob's thin but clear tenor. It sounded better still when they blended with Peter McIntosh, a boy with a guitar (an ancient instrument borrowed from his church) who lived a half mile or so away, but had gravitated to Higgs' Third Street yard like so many of the young musically-inclined of West Kingston.

Like Bob and Bunny, Peter (real name Winston, though he had dropped it long ago) was an immigrant from the rural outback: he had been born on October 19, 1944, in a farm parish in Westmoreland. Like Bob, he had also been abandoned by his father, though not until his mid-teens, at which point Peter's mother had moved her family, out of necessity, to Kingston.

Tosh's voice was a perfect foil for those of Bob and Bunny, being much deeper and richer, and the blend they achieved as a trio could produce wonderful facsimiles of the current US hits on the radio, like the Drifters' Please Stay (with Bob taking the pleading tenor lead) or the Impressions' Gypsy Woman (Bunny's high lead emulating Curtis Mayfield), that would make even the consummate professional Higgs sit up and listen.

Inclined to push his best pupils the hardest, Higgs impressed upon the youthful trio the importance of identifiable material to match their vocal talent. His own philosophy on life – that of a Rastafarian, with a spiritually optimistic, non-violent attitude – earned him respect from neighbourhood youths whose patience usually stretched no further than the end of their ratchet knives. This particularly fascinated Bob Marley, who by natural inclination shared some of Higgs' observe-and-formulate stance. He had (under his family's fundamentalist Christian influence) been wary of Rastas since early childhood, yet Higgs was clearly a kindred spirit and a man who obviously had a handle on life, rotten though the common lot might be, and his lyrics would often deal with injustice and iniquity specific to the Jamaican experience. When he coaxed the youths to write songs, they in turn reflected the way he himself wrote, and Bob's first composition had a philosophic bent to it rather than the more conventional exhortation to dance or romance. Borrowing a familiar epithet of grandfather Omeriah, it was titled Judge Not.

Determined to prove his worth as a writer and singer – to himself, his brothers-in-harmony and his tutor – Bob slowly worked up the courage necessary to visit Musik City record shop and audition himself and Judge Not to Clement Dodd. On his first visit, Coxsone happened not to be on the premises and, when the adrenaline remained sufficiently high to propel Bob on to Beverley's, a record shop owned by a younger producer of Chinese extraction named Leslie Kong, he was brought to earth with a bump by being scornfully ejected by (the also absent) Kong's co-owner brothers.

Bob's determination, however, was re-kindled by an accident at work which made him equally determined to quit the welder's yard rapidly and for good. Using a welding torch one afternoon without wearing protective goggles, some tiny fragments of sharp metal lodged in one of his eyes. The pain was far more than Cedella's hot and cold compresses and herbal potion could deal with and, following a sleepless night in near agony, his mother took him to Kingston Public

---

Top: Joe Higgs, a seminal influence on Marley
Centre: Early ska rocker Prince Buster
Bottom: The smoking of ganja by Rastas took on a ritual, almost religious significance
Opposite: Looking more Motown than Trench Town, the Wailers circa 1965 with (l to r) Bunny Livingston, Bob Marley and Peter Tosh

Hospital the next morning. It took two out-patient visits on successive days, and a lot of careful, painful probing by a doctor, to remove the embedded fragments. The injured eye remained in a delicate condition for some weeks, being at first heavily bandaged and then covered by a protective patch as it slowly healed. Bob saw the incident as a definite omen that his life was veering away from its appointed direction.

Shortly after his accident, Bob was freshly encouraged by talking to fellow welding apprentice Desmond Dekker, who had succeeded where Bob had so far failed, by getting himself an audition at Federal Studios and then actually cutting a single of his own composition, Honour Your Mother And Father. Teenagers were being heard and recorded, said Dekker; at Federal he'd also met a slightly younger boy named James Chambers, whom Leslie Kong had now recorded.

By early in 1962, when Bob, Bunny and Peter (who tinkered with his name again, shortening his surname to 'Tosh', which it would there-after remain) had started to get themselves known around West Kingston by entering talent nights and amateur shows as the Teenagers, in collaboration with another harmonising neighbour named Junior Braithwaite, both Desmond Dekker's single and James Chambers' topi-cal debut Hurricane Hattie (released under the name Jimmy Cliff, with which Chambers has stuck throughout his career) had become Jamaican hits. Dekker introduced Marley to Cliff and, having heard Bob sing, the latter suggested that they should see Leslie Kong together, so that Cliff could make the introduction. A nervous audition, not helped by Kong's abrasive, man-in-a-hurry attitude, ensued at Beverley's record shop, with Bob singing Judge Not totally unaccompanied. It was enough to convince Kong that he had a recordable commodity, and Bob was whisked around to Ken Khouri's Federal Studios, where a four-piece session band learned the song on the spot and a single was made. In the space of a couple of days, Bob cut pretty well his whole repertoire of

recently-written songs for Leslie Kong in similar fashion. Then, with enough material for a couple of potential singles under his belt, Kong had the 16-year-old sign a release form, and handed over £20 in cash as payment for the material. This was to be the only financial reward Bob Marley ever got to see for his initial recordings, but such aggravation was almost immaterial beside the fact that this deal had finally gotten him on to the all-important first recording rung. Judge Not quickly appeared as a single on Kong's Beverley's label (which, presumably due to the producer's carelessness, initially credited 'Bob Morley'), followed during the spring of 1962 by two further efforts, Terror and One Cup Of Coffee – the latter with another odd credit, Bobby Martell. None of them made the Jamaican charts, or got widely heard at the time outside of the Trench Town community who knew who Bob Marley was, but their very existence was sufficient to realise one of Bob's immediate ambi-tions. He left the welding shop for good.

Amazingly, two of these seminal singles were also issued in the UK about a year later, though hardly anyone noticed at the time, least of all Bob Marley, who would almost certainly have had no inkling that Leslie Kong had licensed both Judge Not and One Cup Of Coffee to the tiny London-based independent label Island Records, operated by an Anglo-Jamaican named Chris Blackwell. This low-key setup served mainly to supply music to Britain's burgeoning immigrant West Indian population, with sales at a steady, though unspectacular, level. All the same, both Bob Marley singles (and his name was correctly spelled on the Island pressing of Judge Not) probably sold more in Britain than within the still-fledgling Jamaican record market. This early, tenuous link between Marley and Blackwell was unremarkable at the time. A decade or so later, the combination of Island, Blackwell and Marley would be the launching pad of the latter's international success.

Disillusioned with Leslie Kong once it became clear that he was never to see any further benefit from the three Beverley's singles, Bob refused to cut any more tracks with the pushy producer, and concen-trated again on the vocal group, now expanded to a sextet with the addition of female backup vocalists Beverly Kelso and Cherry Green.

There was also expansion going on at 19 Second Street. During 1962, Cedella became pregnant with a second child, by Toddy Livingston, and began to hanker for somewhere better to live. Her thoughts turned to the USA, and particularly the town of Wilmington,

Channel One Studios in Kingston, one of the many small-time operations that made up the Jamaican recording scene crucial to the development of ska, rock-steady and reggae

Living in conditions of comparative poverty was – and indeed is – the norm for many ordinary Jamaicans

Delaware, where some relatives already lived. Late in the year, she procured passports for both herself and Bob, initially registering her son as 'Nesta Robert Marley' as was still her habit, but being advised by the processing official to reverse the two forenames, Robert being the less ambiguous. Anyway, Robert now insisted on being known as Bob.

A brief visit to her US-based relatives while she was still pregnant made up Cedella's mind – she did not want to raise her second child in the violence and deprivation of Trench Town. Toddy Livingston backed her up, though he had no intention of moving himself, even after Ciddy gave birth to their daughter. The baby girl was named Claudette, though everyone called her Pearl. Since she was half-sister to both Bob and Bunny, it increased the bond between the two teenagers – who were, in any case, far more preoccupied with their singing than about domestic arrangements. Bob was notably non-committal about moving to

the States, and it dawned on Ciddy that he was quite likely not going to leave with her.

Initially, anyway, Ciddy could only afford to move herself to Delaware. She delayed departure until Pearl was old enough, at nine months, to remain temporarily with her sister Edith before being sent for when Ciddy was established in the States. She hoped that Bob would follow at a similar time; for the moment, it was understood that he would remain on Second Street with Toddy and Bunny, an arrangement which suited the now 18-year-old youth just fine.

Things took a turn for the worse domestically, however, when Toddy found it impossible to maintain the rent on the yard room without Cedella's support. He was forced to relocate, and so, forcibly, was Bob, who found himself dossing with friends on a piecemeal basis, before finding a regular night-time squat in the corner of a First Street kitchen along with his friend Vincent Ford (who would share the writing credit, and the royalties, on No Woman, No Cry several years later, after developing serious diabetes). Most meals were the food shared around of an evening during the group practices with Joe Higgs.

During mid-1963 Clement Dodd decided to build his own studio in Kingston. Officially the Jamaica Recording and Publishing Studio Ltd, it became universally known by the much snappier name of Studio One. In the late summer, Bob and friends got the chance to audition there for Dodd, who had plans to launch a new Coxsone Records label built around a fresh roster of talent. With a name switch from the Teenagers to the Wailers (since some of them wouldn't be in their teens for much longer, but all were now proficient wailers both solo and ensemble), they got heard partially through Higgs, who knew the producer, and partly through the help of Alvin 'Franseeco' Patterson, another Rastafarian musician who frequented the yard sessions. Some years older than the young vocalists, he was a virtuoso drummer in the stickless, traditional burru style, who would one day become the Wailers' full-time percussionist.

The Wailers' audition, agreed after Franseeco's glowing advance report of their abilities, was only a middling success, their extreme nervousness undoing the proficiencies honed by hard rehearsal. They concentrated on a couple of their Impressions-influenced harmony soul ballads, but also threw in as a closer their newest (and most sparsely-rehearsed) song, Simmer Down, written by Bob. This was a bouncing ska song with a lyric which addressed itself to Jamaican youth, and specifically to the troublesome rude boys, and though it was basically a very simple number, it had a snappy chorus line (the title) and plenty of potential street credibility. Coxsone smelled a hit, so despite being only moderately impressed by everything else he'd heard from the band, he signed the Wailers to a deal (a straight one-off payment for each song they would record; nothing fancy) and organised a recording session within the week.

When the group arrived to cut Simmer Down, they were impressed to discover that Dodd had assembled the cream of the island's ska instrumentalists, known generically as the Skatalites, and including ace guitarist Ernest Ranglin, sax player Rolando Alphonso and pianist Jackie Mittoo. With full instrumental backing and a horn-heavy arrangement by Alphonso, Simmer Down became a pumping, urgent ska rocker, Bob's shrill lead vocal rattling out the admonitory lyric in arresting style. True to Clement Dodd's hunch, the single was an immediate success, getting

cation with that movement, though much of it was playing the outrage factor to win an audience from the rebel fringes generally – precisely the same trick bands like the Rolling Stones and Pretty Things were pulling in the UK at the time. What the Wailers were expressing in these early years of success were the anger and frustration of Jamaica's ghetto poor, of which the rude boys, with no positive outlet for their energies, were merely another, ugly, manifestation. In much later times, it would still be the lot of the disadvantaged, albeit on a much wider scale, which would motivate most of Bob Marley's songwriting.

Clement Dodd took the group firmly under his wing, in the sense that he paid them for each recording (this, of course, meant that he then

strong airplay on both Jamaica's radio stations and selling as quickly as he could press it over the Christmas period and into 1964. In February, it hit No.1 on the Jamaican chart. The group were slightly put out by Coxsone's unauthorised alteration of their name on the label (to the Wailin' Wailers), but they weren't about to argue with the success.

Simmer Down automatically identified the Wailers with the rude boy movement, though it was actually a warning to rudies, whose anti-social activities were starting to become a tangible menace in the ghettoes, exacerbated by strong rum and a nihilistic attitude born of the violent US gangster movies to which they flocked. The connections were real enough, since Bob, Peter, Bunny and Junior interacted with the hooli-gan-inclined fellow youths of their neighbourhoods as a matter of course, and had reputations of their own as tough, no-mess characters. In contrast with slightly later anti-rude hits songs like Prince Buster's Judge Dread and Dandy Livingstone's Rudy, A Message To You, a lot of the Wailers' Coxsone singles over the next couple of years, with rude boy-orientated lyrics, would further cement their image of close identifi-

Left: Jimmy Cliff, who was to have worldwide hits in the late Sixties
Centre: Millie Small in 1964 at the time of her 'Lollipop smash
Right: Dandy Livingstone on UK television's Top Of The Pops

owned it, not them), gave them a £3 apiece weekly retainer, and also bought them stage costumes – in the early days, slick, tight-jacket-and-trousered suits not unlike those being worn by the black US groups on stage, plus pointed leather shoes akin to those of the UK beat group fra-ternity. He also took the still-homeless Bob Marley under his roof, letting him live and work in the studio, and sleep and stow his belongings in a room out back. Since all Bob wanted to do, essentially, was practice gui-tar, write songs and learn more about recording, the situation was fine by him. It was not too long before he became a musical right-hand man to Dodd, working with and tutoring other aspiring acts as well as the Wailers. He listened avidly to the R&B singles and albums which Coxsone still had shipped in regularly from the US, and was adept at spotting numbers which might be covered or adapted for Jamaican consumption, either by the Wailers or by other Dodd acts.

As Coxsone put out a regular stream of singles, the Wailers hit the Jamaican charts several more times in 1964, notably with Junior Braithwaite's It Hurts To Be Alone (the first song they had auditioned for Coxsone) and Bob and Bunny's sequel to it, Lonesome Feeling. They became one of the biggest live attractions on the island, playing concerts and sound system dances to wide acclaim. They were disappointed, therefore, when former record producer and now politician Edward Seaga, in his capacity as Minister of Development, did not consider them – or, indeed, their recording compatriots the Skatalites, who were probably the island's most revered band – for inclusion in a musical 'Jamaica Ska' delegation sent to perform at the 1964 New York World's Fair. Prince Buster and Jimmy Cliff went instead, along with ska dance band Byron Lee & the Dragonaires, and Millie Small, the teenage girl who had just had ska's first international multi-million-selling hit single with My Boy Lollipop – a top 5 hit in both the UK (where it was recorded for Chris Blackwell's Island label) and America. It occurred to the Wailers that they actually represented something of a political embarrassment for the Jamaican establishment, which could not export supposedly rude boy-embracing musicians from Trench Town's worst quarter and hope to make the desired impression on an international audience that Millie and My Boy Lollipop presumably would. The Skatalites, for their part, were excluded because several of the musicians were Rastafarians and smoked ganga, the strong Jamaican marijuana.

Early in 1965, having found initial success, the Wailers were trimmed back to a trio when first Beverly Kelso left (her compatriot Cherry had actually gone the year before), and then Junior Braithwaite departed not only the group but Jamaica itself, emigrating with his parents to Chicago. However, successful singles still flowed from the Studio One presses. As well as their own songs, the Wailers were tackling some material from unusual sources, like the Tom Jones film theme song What's New Pussycat, the Beatles' And I Love Her (Bob was fascinated by Lennon & McCartney's songs, the first contemporary British music he had ever listened to with real interest), and Jr Walker & the All-Stars' Shotgun, rewritten by Bob as Ska Jerk.

Around the time Braithwaite departed, the others first met Rita Anderson. A 17-year-old nurse, she would spot the trio daily as, on the way to Studio One, they walked past the house in Greenwich Park Road where she lived with several brothers and sisters and her Aunt Viola, her parents having gone to England some five years previously. Recognising the members of her favourite group, Rita eventually found the courage to speak to them one morning, and would thereafter frequently strike

Boxer-turned-bodyguard Roy 'Prince Buster' Campbell became a leading producer and performer on the ska scene

up conversations, normally with Peter Tosh, who enjoyed the flirtatious element in these daily meetings – unlike Bob, who was conspicuously offhand. Rita's hidden agenda in speaking to the trio was that she too was a member of a vocal group, the Soulettes, along with her male cousin Constantine Walker and their friend Marlene Gifford. Eventually, she mentioned this fact to Tosh, who persuaded Clement Dodd to check them out. Coxsone, recognising a latent talent, immediately deputised Bob Marley to work on the act's harmonies and presentation, and finding them suitable material. This liaison was not appreciated at all by the Soulettes, who found Bob a severe and easily irritated taskmaster in rehearsal, but it rapidly transpired that his edginess had much to do with Rita herself: he had fallen for her. Curiously unable at first to communicate the fact, he stayed overtly distant and used Bunny as a rather unwilling go-between to send the girl written love notes.

It was not until after Bob had coaxed the Soulettes through their first single I Love You Baby – which, to general gratification, made the charts – that he and Rita began to speak on a one-to-one level about non-recording matters, as Rita tried to penetrate her professed beau's shyness and find out a little more about him. In his makeshift home behind the studio, by way of illustrating the details of his family back-ground, he owned up about a pile of letters which occupied a table-top: they were communications from his mother Cedella in the US, some of them going back a year or more, and the more recent ones showing signs of distress with regard to what he was doing and why he had never replied. He was, he told Rita, simply too busy with the music to attend to letter-writing. She volunteered to take the matter in hand, and effectively became his secretary, beginning by responding to Ciddy's missives. She introduced herself, explaining Bob's lack of contact, and reassuring his mother that Bob's life in music was progressing well.

However, all was not well with Bob. The claustrophobic conditions under which he was living at the studio were starting to get to him; his sleep was constantly disturbed, and he confided in Rita that he believed a duppy, or malevolent undead spirit, was being driven by somebody to hex him. As a Sunday school teacher and committed Christian, Rita had little truck with duppy business, but Bob insisted that she stay overnight with him in the room in question, to try to help him sort out his prob-lem. She agreed to do so, only to wake herself from a terrifying night-mare during the early hours, in the throes of a near-fit which made her violently sick. Rita was drained with shock, while to Bob his point had merely been rather savagely proved. Mutually spooked by their sur-roundings, they jointly concluded that Bob should get away from Coxsone's back room the following night and stop over with Rita – a 'solution' which led, if anything, to an even more terrifying ordeal the following night when, attempting secrecy from Rita's aunt, they were discovered in the same bed together (albeit innocently sleeping) when Sharon, Rita's baby daughter from an earlier liaison, raised a ruckus and, unfortunately, the rest of the household. Bob was ejected by Aunt Viola, more by force of words than anything else, back through the window by which he had entered, and a terrified Rita went with him.

Rita faced up to her aunt the next day, explaining both Bob's predicament and that they were determined to stay together – and that she and Sharon would leave to be with him if need be. Viola, once her temper subsided, recognised the seriousness of this threat and of the couple's affection for each other; she relented and allowed them to con-vert the back yard shack into an additional family bedroom.

As 1965 came to an end, the Wailers were starting to feel more than a little disgruntlement over their relationship with Coxsone. The group had been a walking hit machine for Clement Dodd for nigh-on two years, yet lacked creative freedom in the face of a notoriously dictatorial producer and, even more to the point, they were scarcely less hungry than they had ever been. Money was coming into Studio One from their success and all they were getting out of it were the wages-per-release and the fixed salary established at the time of Simmer Down. There were confrontations with Dodd, which got them nothing but a Christmas bonus payment, and there were threats from both sides which got nobody anything. A fact of life had to be faced: in the Jamaican record industry, the producer was king, and he reaped the rewards. The only way to buck this system was to join it: the Wailers needed to form their own label, and produce and market their own records.

Of the trio, Bob was the only one who saw a possible way of raising the cash necessary for the group to organise its own independent set-up. His thoughts were on what had been the main thrust of his mother's regular letters since her marriage in Delaware to a Wilmington civil ser-vant named Edward Booker. She had sent for Pearl immediately, and exhorted Bob also to join his family for a new life in America. At Christmas 1964, a plane ticket had arrived to help him make up his mind, but Bob, invoking his heavy commitment to the group and its music, had sent it back. A year later, Ciddy was still pleading, and the realisation came to Bob that only in the US was he likely to be able to earn enough money with which to return to Jamaica and steer the Wailers on to their own path. Bunny and Peter offered no viable alterna-tives, and Rita was supportive of Bob's suggestion. She was fazed, how-ever, by the rider he now added: they must marry before he left for the US. Then, if he eventually decided to stay, it would be a simple matter for Rita to join her husband there. She argued that she could not marry without her absent parents' permission – a standpoint taken even more firmly by her aunt. Somehow, by a mixture of sheer persistence, persua-sion and conviction of his sincerity, Bob gained Aunt Viola's somewhat grudging approval. He told Ciddy nothing at all of the proposal, merely that yes, he would come to live in Wilmington in February 1966.

On the morning of February 10th, in a marriage ceremony officiated by a local JP at the home of a friend of the Anderson family, Bob and Rita, aged 21 and 19 respectively, became husband and wife. On February 11th, in a curiously ironic echo of his own father's departure on the day after his wedding, Bob caught a plane to Philadelphia, en route for Wilmington, Delaware. He would, he vowed, be back, but the early Wailers era came to a close on that day, as Bob Marley departed Jamaican soil for the first time in his life.

JAMMIN'

ob Marley spent almost eight months of 1966 in Wilmington, living in the Booker household with Cedella and her husband Edward. He owned up to Ciddy about having married without informing her or asking her blessing for the wedding and, although hurt at first, she soon realised from the way Bob constantly talked about his wife in glowing terms that he had made a serious commitment. Equally serious, as he also made clear to his hosts, was his intention to make money in the US in order to finance his ambitions back home. This saddened Cedella a little; she had hoped that Bob would be remaining with her – or, at least, in America – permanently. It became ever-clearer to her, however, as the months progressed, that he had an urgent sense of his musical destiny back home and could not be persuaded to stay.

As it happened, the Wilmington sojourn was not to provide Bob with the capital he yearned. He worked hard enough to earn it, taking a variety of short-term jobs from night work in a warehouse to dishwashing in a restaurant, and eventually on an assembly line at the Chrysler car factory, but by October 1966 he had been laid off from the latter and, while attempting to apply for social security, had caught the eye of the Delaware Draft. Faced with a request to register, it was clearly time to make a sharp exit, which Bob did – back to Kingston with such small capital as he had amassed during his stay.

The Wailers did not go into abeyance during his absence. Several singles were issued by Coxsone, some of them leftovers from 1965 sessions, and some new compositions like Bunny's sound system anthems Dancing Shoes and Jerk In Time, and his overtly pro-rude boy Let Him Go. Rita's cousin Constantine (commonly known as Dream) deputised Bob's harmony parts on some of the new recordings, while she herself began to provide a female backup voice on certain tracks, filling the shoes of the departed Beverly Kelso.

Previous page, top: Johnny Nash
This page, top: Rasta culture evident at London's Notting Hill Carnival, August 1987
Centre: A Jamaican police warning against ganja smoking
Bottom: Bob Marley
Opposite: His Imperial Majesty Haile Selassie I, Emperor of Ethiopia

While Bob was staying with Cedella, she was disquieted to note that he had started to take an interest in Rastafarianism, an inevitable result of his four years of close interaction with Joe Higgs, Franseeco Patterson and other Rasta musicians. To Bob, as to many of the post-war generation of Jamaican youth who looked around them and saw little but frustration and hopelessness, both the Africa-leaning thoughts of Marcus Garvey and the Rasta concept of a living black deliverer whose power would eventually sweep aside their suffering, held some magnetism. Fundamentalist Christian Cedella rejected the idea completely, having always regarded Rastas as suspicious outcasts of society. When mother and son argued these views, Ciddy's only consolation was that even the Rastafarian philosophy was better than the ruinous criminal street element into which she had feared her son had fallen, bearing in mind the rude boy identification with much of the Wailers' music.

Ironically, an event which dramatically raised the Rastafarian currency in Jamaica (with the population as a whole, if not with the people who actually controlled the island) took place while Bob was absent from his homeland. During April 1966, Emperor Haile Selassie of Ethiopia made a three-day state visit to Jamaica. Though he was invited by the government, which organised an official programme, it was the devout Rasta community and the Jamaican poor in general, fascinated by the possibility that this might actually be the black messiah and a hope of deliverance, who turned the Emperor's arrival on Jamaican soil into one of the most spectacular events the island had ever witnessed. The announcement of the date and time when Selassie's plane was to touch down at Palisadoes Airport, ten miles or so south-east of Kingston, drew upwards of 100,000 people, a huge proportion of them regarding this as a holy pilgrimage. Such was the size and evident fervour of the crowd which flowed across the airport on the morning of April 21, that Selassie was reluctant to leave his plane for some considerable time. He eventually did so after the authorities, finding the official welcoming ceremony impossible to stage under the circumstances, requested Mortimer Planno, a widely respected Rastafarian elder, to address the multitude and appeal for calm and a clear passage for the Emperor to the car which was to take him to the city.

Rita Marley, with some friends, was among the roadside throng which attended Selassie's drive from airport to city. A Christian (in fact, a Sunday school teacher) who had, like Bob, found herself in an environment where the Rasta faith was a constantly-recurring topic, Rita – quite apart from wanting to witness an historic event – privately determined to test a Rasta claim by attempting to see the Emperor at the closest range possible. When the Imperial limousine moved slowly past her vantage point, she experienced – as she excitedly attested to Bob by

Desmond Dekker on British television in 1969 at the time of his huge international hit Israelites

letter later the same day – an intense moment of spiritual awareness. Mentally querying his divine state as she stared at him through the car window, Rita made eye contact with Selassie at the precise second that her unspoken question required its answer – surely an affirmative reply. Moreover, the committed Rastas had told her that Selassie's hands would bear the holy stigmata: the holes that Christ's hands had received from the nails of the cross. As the Emperor simultaneously lifted his hand to wave, Rita noted a deep shadow in the centre of his palm.

Bob arrived back in Kingston to find the local music starting to undergo a change, too. The familiar ska beat which underpinned most uptempo Jamaican hits was slowing down into an easier, bass-driven rhythm which became known as rock steady. When the Wailers reconvened at Studio One, they too would be expected to make some different noises if they wanted to keep up with the way the trends were swinging. However, Bob had a trump card or two up his sleeve, in the shape of a whole notebook of new songs on which he had painstakingly worked with his acoustic guitar during his American exile. Some came directly out of his experiences: the observations he had made in America, and the isolation he had frequently felt.

Bend Down Low and Mellow Mood, a pair of reflective songs which hinted that the Marley muse was becoming simultaneously more personal, but also reaching out to a wider world outside the Wailers' usual audience, were the first two new numbers to be recorded. They were cut at Studio One, but the group, and Bob in particular, were keen to try to bypass Coxsone with the actual release, knowing that it was the only way they stood to make any money out of it. This was what Bob had gone to America for, after all, so the comparatively paltry $700 with which he had returned was put into the creation of a custom label, originally named Wail 'n' Soul 'Em (after its two acts, the Wailers and Rita Marley's Soulettes), and later to be abridged slightly to Wail 'n' Soul. The group also set up (literally, with hammer, nails and wood) a tiny record shop from which to peddle mostly their own recorded wares. This was erected in Greenwich Park Road directly in front of Rita's Aunt Viola's property, with auntie apparently registering her approval by taking a turn with the hammer and nails during construction.

Distribution was a problem, however, as were proper advertising and promotion. All these elements, vital to the success cycle of a single, needed money, a commodity sadly lacking around Wail 'n' Soul 'Em. Coxsone helped out for while in practical ways (though not with

with another rude boy rave, Al Capone, while veteran Jamaican studio outfit the Skatalites reached the British top 50 with their energetic revival of the old movie theme The Guns Of Navarone, which again was a staple dancefloor item through the early summer. The latter single was released in the UK by Chris Blackwell's Island label, which released the Wailers' Bend Down Low (and Tosh's I'm The Toughest) at the same time, without the same sort of success. Back home, the group found themselves, for the moment, left high and dry, with an essentially bankrupt label and, now, no studio deal.

Bob decided to temporarily cut his losses. With the now-pregnant Rita and her daughter Sharon, he exited Kingston and went back to Malcolm country in St. Ann, where the family opened up the cabin which Omeriah (who had died in 1965) had given to Ciddy when Bob was born. Here they could live cheaply but with a far better quality of life than in Trench Town; Bob cultivated a portion of the land which his grandfather had once overseen, and provided food on the table and a little profit through trade, while the occasional trip back to Kingston took care of what performing or business there was to be done. The Wailers cut two more singles in 1967, Nice Time and Hypocrites, with producer Clancy Eccles at Dynamic Studios, both of which were pressed up with Wail 'n' Soul labels for Bob to distribute around Kingston's record shops himself – by bicycle!

money), but withdrew after it became clear to both him and the Wailers that their former arrangement stood little chance of reconvening. Peter Tosh and Bunny Livingston had fallen out with the producer following a showdown incident at Studio One in which the duo had refused to work for nothing on another act's session, and Dodd, declining to take the bait and pull his oft-touted gun on them, had called in the police to get them ejected. He released one more single, Tosh's solo effort I'm The Toughest, probably more as an act of revenge than anything else – since, of course, he paid Peter not a penny out of it.

1967 saw Jamaican music making some international commercial progress, something it had not achieved since My Boy Lollipop early in 1964. Notably, Bob's one-time co-worker Desmond Dekker scored a UK top 20 hit during the summer with 007 (Shanty Town), a tale of Trench Town rude boys whose lyrics meant nothing to the British audience, but whose skanking rock steady rhythm was big on club dancefloors. Sound system DJ Prince Buster also made the top 20 via the hip dancefloors

Top: Robert Nesta Marley
Right: The highly influential producer and singer with a string of hits to his name, Johnny Nash

This slowed-down, rurally-based period in Bob Marley's life proved a key one in the development of his personal and spiritual philosophy. Between working on the land and writing occasional songs (sometimes with Rita), he grew his hair, meditatively puffed on ganga he had grown in his own field and, above all, read his Bible, constantly finding in it the pointers that were ever reinforcing his growing Rastafarian faith. Rita, fired by her encounter with Haile Selassie the previous year, had already become a convert. Soon after they had re-settled in St. Ann, the couple's first child was born – a daughter whom they named Cedella, after her paternal grandmother.

Bunny Livingston, meanwhile, got himself busted by the Kingston police for ganga possession at the end of the year, in somewhat suspect circumstances (he didn't actually have any on him), and spent the next 14 months in jail. He was still on a prison farm when, in mid-1968, Peter Tosh also found himself behind bars following his arrest (alongside Prince Buster) at an anti-Rhodesia rally. Even Bob – with Mortimer

There were various local mystics on the fringes of the Rastafarian and Christian communities in Jamaica, including Prince Emmanuel, who claimed to be the Black Christ

Planno, whom he was consulting frequently and at length about Rastafarianism – got arrested during a visit to Kingston after he let the Rasta elder drive his car without a license. It was a minor misdemeanour which only cost Marley and Planno a night of their liberty, but the incident cemented a period of enforced inactivity by the Wailers.

Mortimer Planno essentially became Bob's manager during 1968, with the singer referring to him constantly on matters of practical as well as spiritual concern. With much of the Wailers' career in abeyance, the latter dominated the Marley energies, and it was during these months that's Bob's Rastafarian faith was finally confirmed, as he flung himself ever more whole-heartedly into studying its tenets. It was at one of the regular Sunday afternoon Rasta Groundations (an extended, intense prayer meeting) in Jones Town that Bob was introduced to the black American vocalist Johnny Nash, who was working in Jamaica at the time with his partner and manager Danny Sims.

Born in 1940, and therefore some five years older than Marley, Nash had been a moderately well-known name, both as a singer and an actor, in the US since the late 1950s, when he had recorded the top 40 hits A Very Special Love and The Teen Commandments (the latter in a trio with Paul Anka and George Hamilton IV) for ABC Paramount Records. After a decade of semi-success, Nash had formed his own label, JAD, in partnership with manager/promoter/publisher Sims, and both were now resident in Jamaica and recording at Federal studios – with imported US musicians and production (by Nash's other partner, Arthur Jenkins), but making music on which Jamaican rhythms had strongly rubbed off. Nash's first Kingston-cut single, Hold Me Tight, was an almost immediate top 5 hit (his first) in Britain in the early autumn, and attained equal status in the US within a month, re-establishing his career at a new international peak. It would be followed by two more major hits from the same sessions, You Got Soul and a revival of Sam Cooke's Cupid, and all three carried a distinctive, grooving rock steady rhythm that was wholly Jamaican in feel.

Nash's revival was just breaking when he met Bob, heard him sing a couple of songs, and insisted that he audition for Danny Sims, who was suitably astounded by the quality and quantity of the largely recently-written and unrecorded Marley repertoire. Bob also familiarised Sims with the Wailers' music, and introduced him to Peter Tosh (Bunny was still in jail at the time), which further enthused Sims and Nash's interest. A deal was struck whereby Sims signed all three Wailers as songwriters, with himself representing their worldwide publishing interests. Nash would have first pick of the material they wrote under the deal, and JAD would finance all the band's studio sessions to provide demo recordings. In view of the security this arrangement brought, after a period of frustrating struggle, it was little wonder that the three Wailers embraced it eagerly. An additional advantage was that the material they were providing for JAD was primarily directed at the US/UK market, for which the deal anticipated songs in a soul/rock steady mould; it left them with some freedom to record material more specifically tailored for the local audience under their own auspices, the only stipulation being that these singles would only be released in the Caribbean.

Towards the end of 1968, the word reggae first appeared in the Jamaican music vocabulary. In fact, it initially appeared as Do The Reggay on Toots & the Maytals's Leslie Kong-produced single of the same title, which referred specifically to a new dance rhythm, but the accepted spelling was quickly adopted as a description of the new, more subtle and sinuous beat, with an over-active burbling bass-line and almost trance-like ticking rhythm guitar, which took over wholesale in the productions coming from Kong at Beverley's Records, and from Lee Perry's Upsetter productions. Once again, it was Bob Marley's one-time soul mate Desmond Dekker who spearheaded its international drive, when his Kong-produced Israelites, a classic Jamaican sufferer's lament with lyrics near-incomprehensible to British and American audiences, but a hot rhythm track that startled with its originality, exploded as an international hit. At the end of April 1969, it became the first Jamaican single ever to reach No.1 in the UK, and by the end of June, it was also in the US top 10. Although it was to be Dekker's only American success, it launched him – and reggae music in general – into a lengthy hit streak in Britain. Dekker's other UK hits in 1969/70 included top tenners with It Mek and You Can Get It If You Really Want, and he was followed high in the charts by Jimmy Cliff's Wonderful World, Beautiful People (which also made the US top 30), the Kong-produced Long Shot (Kick De Bucket) by the Pioneers, Young, Gifted And Black and Pied Piper from Bob (Andy) and Marcia (Griffiths), studio group the Harry J All-Stars with The Liquidator, Boris Gardiner with Elizabethan Reggae, and Lee Perry's house band the Upsetters with Return Of Django.

Busy as they were with their writing and demoing for JAD, the Wailers had no intention of letting this hot wind of change on the local scene pass them by. Still with little immediate prospect of reactivating their own label, the group linked up for recording with Leslie Kong, thus fulfilling Bob's prediction to Kong that they would one day work together again. It isn't clear whether, at the time, either man referred back to the second half of that prophecy, which was that Kong would never reap any benefit from the second association, but the sessions at Dynamic Studios seem to have been relatively uneventful and unmarked by any kind of strife between producer and group. Ten songs were recorded, including Caution, Do It Twice and Soul Shakedown Party, all notable updates on the Wailers' mid-1960s sound, and a chance for them to get back into the local groove after some months of tailor-writing for JAD. The subsequent parting was amicable, leaving Kong with several likely singles and the group with a modicum of finance.

During the middle six months of 1969, including the period when Desmond Dekker's Israelites was storming the US chart, Bob had another working exile in Delaware, again with the express intention of raising some capital. Stints back on the car assembly line and at assorted evening pick-up jobs were alleviated by the songwriting he did while living again at his mother's house. In the long run, he returned to Jamaica with a legacy of songs more valuable than the moderate bankroll which came back with him. The group recognised this, and again putting label plans aside, resolved to get the new material on record as soon as possible.

Once more they sought a producer, and this time passed over Leslie Kong in favour of the equally hot mastermind of the Upsetters' overseas success, Lee 'Scratch' Perry – actually an old acquaintance from Clement Dodd's studio back in the early rude boy days. Perry, while an occasionally volatile character, had a more positive production attitude than Kong – he saw the Wailers for their still unfulfilled potential rather than as another helping of singles fodder, and took the moulding of their sound in hand, much as one-time mentor Coxsone had done. Perry brought in a harder lead vocal edge in place of the traditional three-part harmonies, and he also gave the Wailers a dynamic new instrumental underpinning by teaming them with his hot house band, the Upsetters.

Previously known as the Hippy Boys when backing Max Romeo (of pornographic hit Wet Dream fame), the Upsetters revolved around their diamond-hard rhythm section: Aston 'Family Man' Barrett on bass and his younger brother Carlton (universally known as 'Carlie') Barrett on drums, with Alva Lewis handling guitar, and Glen Adams on keyboards. The chemistry which arose between these musicians and the Wailers was immediately apparent and, in particular, the mutual musical bond between Bob Marley and the Barrett brothers would remain solid for the remainder of Bob's life.

The Wailers, Perry and the Upsetters started working together in the studio towards the end of 1969, attempting some of the songs Bob had written during his most recent American sojourn, some stripped down and rebuilt versions of earlier group numbers, and some new material on which Marley and Perry collaborated. Notable songs which emerged were Soul Rebel (cut earlier as a JAD demo), the horror tale Mr. Brown, and the assertive Duppy Conqueror. A second series of sessions took place early in 1970, which produced probably the group's most effective and forward-looking material yet: songs like Small Axe, Sun Is Shining, Kaya, Don't Rock My Boat and Lively Up Yourself.

The group still hoped to get their own label off the ground with this material and, with the limited finances available, Tuff Gong records was initiated on a shoestring to release Duppy Conquerer as a single. Unfortunately, the label imploded from precisely the same kind of mal-nourishment as Wail 'n' Soul before it, and the Wailers philosophically agreed to their work with Perry being released on his Upsetter label. Via this arrangement, several of the songs, like Soul Rebel and Duppy Conqueror, re-established the group at Sound System level – though they badly wanted, as ever, for Jamaican radio airplay and the more solid sales this exposure generated.

At the end of 1970, Bob travelled to Sweden. He went at the invitation of Danny Sims in order to join Johnny Nash in Stockholm to work on soundtrack songs for a locally-made movie titled Love Is Not A Game, in which Nash had a leading role and also the music rights. For some weeks, with freezing Scandinavian weather outside, Bob, Johnny and Nash's keyboards player John 'Rabbit' Bundrick worked in hotel rooms on assorted collaborations (and, according to Bundrick, a large number of Swedish girls), until the project suddenly came to a halt when the money ran out – the film was apparently finished, but never saw a release, and its soundtrack music (Bob and Rabbit co-wrote the title song) seems to be lost forever. Bob returned to Jamaica, departing Sweden at mid-loggerheads with Danny Sims, and (again according to Bundrick) took Johnny Nash's guitar and tape recorder with him in lieu of a financial settlement.

Back in Jamaica in the spring of 1971, the Wailers regrouped once again and resumed recording, this time using Harry J's and Dynamic studios. Though they were no longer working with Lee Perry, the group held on to the Barrett brothers rhythm section from his old house band: the symbiosis was now too strong to break. New keyboards player Tyrone Downie, a mere 15 years old but already a respected name on the Kingston live circuit, was recruited in place of the Barretts' previous colleague Glen Adams, now emigrated to the US. Material recorded included several future Jamaican singles, like Lick Samba, Craven Choke Puppy and, most significantly, the socially aware and assertive Trench Town Rock which, for a change, was a celebration of the spirit of the ghetto rather than a put-down of its injustices. Perhaps for this reason, the song became the Wailers' biggest Jamaican hit for years.

They also had a new manager and general overseer in the form of Alan 'Skill' Cole, a charismatic Jamaican soccer star who got on well with Bob because of their mutual Rasta leanings and also their joint addiction to football. Skill was also ostensibly now their producer, though in fact the new recordings were produced by Bob and the band under the collective Tuff Gong banner.

In the early autumn, Bob, Peter and Bunny, plus Carlie and Family Man Barrett, departed for England, again at the behest of Danny Sims, and again – on the face of it – for something extremely positive: Johnny Nash had secured a new recording contract with the UK branch of CBS Records, which was provisionally interested in signing the Wailers as well. Sims wanted them to play back-up on the London sessions for

Lee 'Scratch' Perry, a pioneering spirit in Jamaican record production who made a crucial contribution to the Wailers' records

Nash's next album, which would contain several Marley songs, and support him on a UK tour. There was a good chance that they would cut some material of their own, too.

Some of this came to pass, some didn't. The sessions for Nash's album took place in London during October, with the material cut including Bob's songs Stir It Up, Guava Jelly, Comma Comma and (co-written with Nash) You Poured Sugar On Me. With Nash acting as producer, the Wailers also recorded four songs of their own, the most notable being Reggae On Broadway, a heavy funk/reggae hybrid.

Although CBS had provisionally agreed to finance a joint Nash/Wailers promotional tour, only sporadic club gigs ever came about for the full group. Bob joined Johnny and a backup band led by Rabbit Bundrick for a low-key 18-day school and college tour which took them all over the UK, but it was not what anybody had originally had in mind. Eventually, at the end of the year, when Nash and Sims left for New York to sort out the details of the former's US recording deal, the Wailers

were left in the care of Brent Clarke, a freelance London record promotion man of Caribbean extraction whom Sims had appointed their temporary European manager. With no sign of a record release from CBS, the group were spending their days rehearsing in a music publisher's basement studio, and their evenings in a communal house in Neasden or around London's pubs. Most importantly, they were not earning any money, and did not have the price of the airfare home. Prevailed upon (particularly by Bunny Livingston, who felt himself slowly going insane in the winter climate, parted from his girlfriend) to help move things along, Clarke set up a meeting at Island Records with Chris Blackwell. It would possibly be the single most important decision taken throughout the Wailers' entire career.

Above: Bob Marley in action in 1973, swopping his usual guitar for the percussion sound of the conga drum

THE YEARS OF FAME

Right person, right place, right time. Chris Blackwell was perhaps the one UK record industry man who would not have turned the Wailers away. Brent Clarke approached him with an armful of recordings and a potted history of the group's Caribbean success to date, but Blackwell didn't really need the history lessons. He was, and had been for years, a close observer of the Jamaican music industry, and although it had been a long time since Island had last licensed a Wailers single for the UK (Bend Down Low in 1967), he was familiar with their music, as well as the fact that they had virtually lurched unguided from hit to hit and crisis to crisis for nigh-on a decade, and yet now appeared to be more accomplished than ever.

By the time Blackwell and Marley met face-to-face, the former had decided to go out on a limb with the Wailers. His main reservation had been the difficult reputation with which transatlantic hearsay had landed the group, yet Bob gave all the signs of being a serious, committed musician, albeit one presently stuck in a deep, dark hole. Blackwell also had the notion that Island could probably make something of the Wailers as an album act, as it had with the many rock acts – Free, Traffic, Cat Stevens and others – which Blackwell had signed in recent years. In Jamaica, albums tended to be merely belated compilations of singles tracks – Lee Perry had already anthologised two batches of his Wailers recordings in this way as the LPs Soul Rebels and Soul Revolution – but there was nothing cast in stone which said that reggae could not be conceived and recorded in a coherent album form. With the knowledge that he would have to disentangle them from Danny Sims and the JAD deal in the fairly short term, Blackwell was nonetheless willing to advance the Wailers sufficient money – £8,000 was the sum negotiated with Brent Clarke – to return home and start recording material for a debut Island album. Moreover, the Wailers' precarious Tuff Gong concern would finally be secure: the deal would

Previous page, top: Bob Marley in action at London's Lyceum Ballroom in 1975
This page, top: Island founder and supremo Chris Blackwell
Centre: Bob Marley
Bottom: Motown superstar Stevie Wonder, January 1974 at the Rainbow Theatre, London

allow them to control the release of their material on their own label within Jamaica itself.

The group returned home with their spirits transformed from the depths of despair to the height of optimism – notably Bunny's, who joyfully upped and left his Trench Town accommodation and resettled in Rasta-favoured Bull Bay, along the coast. The group immediately went into rehearsal and through the first months of 1972, working variously at Harry J's and Dynamic studios, produced a dozen or so tracks for possible album inclusion. Some were re-workings of items originally cut the previous year for Jamaican singles, like Bob's Concrete Jungle and Midnight Ravers, and Peter's Stop That Train, while other songs were first-time runs on new compositions. The group also recut Stir It Up, one of the tracks written by Bob on which they had backed Johnny Nash the previous year.

By the late spring, the master tapes were ready, and Bob flew them to London personally for delivery to Chris Blackwell. Ironically, when he arrived, Johnny Nash's single, Stir It Up, had been released and was in the UK chart, where it peaked at No.14. On the other hand, the Wailers' Reggae On Broadway, which followed from CBS a couple of months later, got little promotion and flopped completely.

At Island's Basing Street studios, with Bob in attendance much of the time, Chris Blackwell systematically remixed and subtly re-jigged the Wailers' original Jamaican masters into the coherent overall mood of a genuine album. Judicious overdubbing – of lead lines by American guitarist Wayne Perkins, for example, on three of the tracks, and keyboard sweetening by Rabbit Bundrick on most of them – provided the all-important finishing touches.

Before the planned release of the album at the end of the year, Blackwell needed to address the question of the Wailers' contract. The CBS legal department was already referring Island to the existing deal with Danny Sims' company Cayman Music, of which CBS Records was the recording beneficiary. Bob himself met Sims to discover on what terms he would release the Wailers from their existing agreement. For his part, Sims was aware that CBS in London was not keen to release any more Marley material, despite his own urging, so he offered a new deal whereby, in return for Bob, Bunny and Peter re-signing as songwriters with Cayman Music, which would mean Sims controlling their publishing income, Island could buy out the group's existing contract for £5,000 plus a suitable sum to repay advances and expenses from CBS. Sims also required two per cent of the profits on the Wailers' first six Island albums. These terms were phoned to Blackwell, who concurred, eager to clear the way for release of the album, now given the title Catch A Fire.

Released in April 1973 on both sides of the Atlantic, the album received excellent reviews in the music press, particularly the *Melody Maker* in the UK, and *Rolling Stone* in America. It did not chart in either country, but Chris Blackwell knew that it would take a couple more such well-received albums and an awful lot of promotion and hard touring before the Wailers reached a sufficiently large audience to start having hit records. As soon as Catch A Fire had been completed, Blackwell gave the group notice to get to work on its follow-up, and indeed much

clubs and small provincial theatres. It was the most gruelling period of ongoing live work the Wailers had so far undertaken, and from a somewhat uncertain and scrappy start, they had clicked into tight musical efficiency by the time the trek was over, the main problem (apart from being roadie-less and therefore having to hump their own gear in and out of every venue) being maintaining a diet acceptable to a Rastafarian in a land which to them was utter culinary Babylon. They got through it, but the particularly fastidious Bunny Livingston was practically starving

of another album had been laid down at Harry J's studio before the Wailers left for London in April 1973 to finally undertake their first proper tour of the UK.

The group toured Britain as a sextet, with new keyboards player Earl 'Wire' Lindo joining the three vocalists and the Barrett brothers on the road. Lindo was ostensibly hired just for this tour and the follow-up trek across America, but in fact he would remain a Wailer for a fair proportion of the band's life.

The British tour, financed by Island with promotion of Catch A Fire the main criterion, was a hard-slog 90-day affair, beginning in London and criss-crossing the entire country as far as Belfast, taking in mainly

Bob Marley and the Wailers on UK television's Old Grey Whistle Test, 1973, performing Concrete Jungle from their Catch A Fire album

by the time they returned to London, with its wider availability of West Indian food, in the early summer.

In some ways, the most notable aspect of the tour was the way in which it centred Bob, already the chief songwriter, vocalist and major driving force, as the focus of the band. They were not billed yet as 'Bob Marley & the Wailers', but in England, that was generally the way they were visualised. The fact was not lost on Bob, who felt comfortable being in control, and certainly not on Peter and Bunny, who believed this was the way Chris Blackwell was setting things up (probably true), and felt somewhat aggrieved about it. A combination of the food and temperature problem and a growing loathing of the road in general and flying in particular, plus disgruntlement over the Wailers' evolving structure, had just about done for Bunny by late June, when they finally touched down again on Jamaican soil. Before escaping to his coastal

Blackwell and renamed Island House, the intention being for it to serve as the label's Jamaican HQ now that Blackwell had re-committed himself to the island's music since signing the Wailers. He offered the group free usage of the place, and almost immediately lost control of it in practical terms, since Bob and cohorts moved in en masse and reinvented it as the Wailers' Jamaican HQ.

Just before their second Island album was released, the Wailers returned to America, having been given a support slot on a tour by Sly &

hideaway, he informed Bob that although he would continue studio work and Jamaican gigs, as far as the wider world went, he had just quit. He had no intention of ever touring as a Wailer again.

With a shorter but all-important American tour close on the horizon, Bunny's decision spelled a problem for the Wailers, which Bob and Peter solved in the short term by contacting Joe Higgs, who agreed to take Bunny's vocal slot on the US trek, currently being organised by Lee Jaffe, a white American friend of Bob who had met him through Island's New York office, and who played blues harmonica in a manner which Marley greatly admired.

The US tour, again mainly club dates, began early in July, taking in Boston, New York (where the Wailers were co-billed with fellow novice Bruce Springsteen, and where Bob's mother and family came to see a show), the mid-west, Florida, and finally California. It closed in San Francisco and, road-weary, the band flew home.

Home in Kingston for the band by mid-1973 tended to be a large house at 56 Hope Road, in an upmarket area not far from the Prime Minister's official residence. The mansion had been bought by Chris

World famous photographers who captured the visual magic of Marley included Annie Leibovitz (left) and David Redfern (right)

the Family Stone, the top US black act of the time. Trouble was, they were too good, too crowd-pleasing by half. After being upstaged at four concerts in a row, Stone had them thrown off the tour, and once again the Wailers were stranded in a foreign country with little visible means of support. They did make it to San Francisco though, to play an important, widely influential live FM radio broadcast, before flying home.

In mid-November, the Burnin' album, a grittier overall picture of the Wailers' music, was released, again incorporating new versions of some earlier songs (like Small Axe and Duppy Conqueror) with newly-written material such as Bunny's stirring Hallelujah Time and Pass It On, and a trio of activist anthems from Bob: Burnin' And Lootin', I Shot The Sheriff and Get Up, Stand Up, the latter destined to become a regular in-concert crowd-rouser. The LP was just in the shops in Britain when the Wailers

Marley injected the normally laid-back approach of most reggae musicians with an on-stage dynamic befitting the world's rock stadia

flew in again for a promotional trek, this time as a quintet: Bunny had not changed his stance and Joe Higgs had had enough of the road life – Bob and Peter made up a dual-vocal front line. The early gigs, opening in Nottingham, were all in the northern half of Britain, and cold, snowy weather set in early, sapping the band's morale to a dangerous level. Eventually, with eleven days still left on the itinerary, Peter Tosh had a blazing row with Bob and promptly left the band, possibly acting as the catalyst for Wire Lindo, who announced that he too was quitting to fly to the States and play with Taj Mahal. This débâcle did Burnin' no harm: again it was positively reviewed – in fact, favourably compared to Catch A Fire by writers who appreciated the rootsier, less glossy and over-dubbed edge shown in this selecton of Wailers' music. Sales, while again not of chartmaking proportions, built steadily upon those of its predecessor. What was much more significant was that it marked the

end of the original Wailers as a regular performing unit – although they would still do a couple more Jamaican concert together, including one six months later in May 1974 when they supported Motown superstar Marvin Gaye at a benefit show in Kingston. This concert, with some new songs added, was similar to that given by the Wailers overseas in 1973, but was a new experience for the Jamaican audience, who discovered that the one-time ska vocal group had developed something of a big-time rock band persona, and that Bob Marley had become a charismatic figure on stage, the undoubted leader of the band.

After the Gaye concert, Bob was sought out by Don Taylor, a Jamaican who had emigrated to the States some years previously and gotten involved as a general hustler in the music business, road managing a stream of big-name R&B acts like Martha & the Vandellas and Little Anthony & the Imperials. At present part of Marvin Gaye's tour entourage, he very much wanted to manage Marley and the Wailers, and gave Bob a lengthy line of smart talk which made it clear why he was the man for the currently vacant position. Bob was impressed by Taylor's connections, his enthusiasm and his sheer bare-faced cheek, all of which would appear to stand a potential manager in good stead. After some thought, and consultation by Bob with his confidante and lawyer Diane Jobson, Taylor was offered the job.

Much of the year was spent preparing and recordings songs for the next album, and attempting to formulate the new structure of the Wailers now that Bunny and Peter had both written themselves out of the picture. The core of the band was now Bob and Carlie and Family Man Barrett, and recording sessions for new songs like Talkin' Blues, Knotty Dread and Road Block involved principly this trio, with Lee Jaffe playing occasional harmonica, teenage studio player Bernard 'Touter' Harvey adding keyboards where required, and vocal harmonies coming from Rita Marley with her friends Marcia Griffiths and Judy Mowatt – who were already starting to be referred to as the I-Threes, under which name they would shortly be integrated fully into the performing version of the band. Without Peter Tosh there was no lead guitar player, a fact which Bob took philosophically, knowing that a session man could eventually be mixed in when the tapes were delivered to Island.

Road Block, an angry observation about the social state of Jamaica, and particularly its police, was based on an actual stop-and-search incident in which Bob and some companions were involved, and was released as a single specifically for Jamaica on the now up-and-running Tuff Gong label. It struck an immediate local chord and sold hugely, though appeared to be the subject of a nervous radio ban until an exasperated Marley took matters into his own hands and personally intimidated some DJs into reflecting the record's success (Skill Cole, accompanying him to the JBC studios, meaningfully cradled a baseball bat as Bob made his 'appeal' for airplay).

Most of Bob's newer songs, plus updates of earlier favourites Bend Down Low and Lively Up Yourself, and the Trench Town sentimental No Woman, No Cry, on which Bob had been working for some time, made it on to the album, which was completed by August of 1974. Its title was to have been Knotty Dread, after one of the songs, but along the way to release it transmuted slightly into Natty Dread, which Blackwell felt would have more universal appeal – even though this destroyed the sense of the title in the context of its song (in the Jamaican accent, the two words sounded the same). The album's final mix took place in London, and the required guitarist was found in the shape of Al Anderson, an American blues/rock player who was doing sessions at Island studios on guitar and bass after a spell playing in the UK with John Martyn. Bob was impressed by Anderson's natural blues styling, and asked him to come to Jamaica and join the Wailers.

Marley with the projected image of Rastafarian icon Emperor Haile Selassie I as a stage backdrop

Several delays over the album's release meant that although it was finished before the end of the autumn, it was to be held over for early 1975 release. Bob's biggest commercial success of 1974, meanwhile, was as a songwriter, thanks to Eric Clapton's cover version of a song from Burnin', I Shot The Sheriff. Originally cut as a track for Clapton's 461 Ocean Boulevard album, the song was extracted as a single during the summer, initially peaking at No.9 in the UK chart, then going on to reach No.1 in the US a couple of weeks later. Despite other widely-heard cover versions of Marley songs by the likes of Johnny Nash and Barbra Streisand, this major international success by one of rock music's most exalted artists was the biggest advertisement yet that Bob Marley's songwriting prowess – and to some extent reggae music itself, since Clapton's version kept closely to the rhythm and spirit of the original – had received in the world at large.

Natty Dread was released in January 1975, credited very significantly to Bob Marley & the Wailers. In fact, an intense portrait of Bob filled virtually the entire front sleeve (designed by Jamaican artist Neville Garrick, who had made the original Tuff Gong logo for Bob, and was now on board as the organisation's full-time creator of visuals and graphics). It was obviously no coincidence that this month was when

the official announcement that the three original Wailers had parted company was made to the world at large. Bunny and Peter had often been around to observe Natty Dread recording sessions, but had taken no part in them, and both were now actively pursuing songwriting, recording and label plans of their own.

Playing a concert alongside US visitors the Jackson 5, shortly after the album release, Bob had a chance to test the new-look Wailers as a stage unit, with the harmonising I-Threes as a vocal counterpoint to himself leading at stage front. Al Anderson, who had been in Jamaica for some months now, also made his mark firmly on lead guitar. Touter Harvey, who had played on the Natty Dread sessions, was on keyboards, though not destined to remain there for long, since Bob was aware that the young teenager didn't have the stamina or experience to survive the rigours of overseas touring, and he and Family Man were working on persuading Tyrone Downie, tucked away playing with a tourist hotel band at the time, to fill the vital keyboards role.

The knitted 'rasta hat' became a fashion essential among fans worldwide after being popularised by Marley and other reggae stars

After a period of difficulty between Bob and Chris Blackwell, the fallout from which had helped delay the release of Natty Dread, the two men came to a new understanding which also resulted in the Marley clan and Bob's Tuff Gong recording set-up taking over Island House on Hope Road, which would remain the centre of Wailers activity in Jamaica for the rest of Bob's life (and, indeed, beyond – in the 1990s it still functions as the Bob Marley Museum, one of Kingston's major tourist attractions).

Bob pursued a brief but interesting sideline to his own burgeoning career during May 1975, when he collaborated on the making of an album with the white American singer/songwriter Martha Velez, who had been in the hit Broadway production of *Hair*. She came to Harry J's studio in Jamaica to record the project, which was co-produced by Bob and Lee Perry, with most of the Wailers playing on the sessions and the I-Threes providing backup vocals. Five of Bob's own songs were recorded, including Disco Night, which he co-wrote with Martha during the early stages of recording. The album, entitled Escape From Babylon, was to be a modest chart success (reaching No.153) in the US exactly a year later, at the same time that Bob & the Wailers were also enjoying their first major US album chart success.

By the middle of the year, when Don Taylor in his first major management assignment had finalised a US tour, the Wailers possessed the line-up to tackle it. The I-Threes were officially on board, Tyrone Downie was in the band, and so was Seeco Patterson, the Wailers' mentor from their pre-Coxsone days, whom Bob had persuaded to fill out the stage sound with a variety of percussion.

The 1975 American tour was to be the band's biggest overseas trek yet. Lasting nearly a month, it took in a host of major North American cities, from Canada down to California. Even though they were still

mainly playing clubs and smaller venues, the Wailers drew packed houses, and noted that everywhere they performed they were drawing, alongside a young white rock audience alerted by album reviews in the likes of *Rolling Stone*, heavy attendance from expatriot Jamaican communities, turning out, as it were, to cheer the home team on tour. In New York, an extra impromptu show was arranged, immediately selling out, and the same thing happened in San Francisco. In Chicago, Bob met up again with one-time Wailer Junior Braithwaite, who by now had been living in the States for ten years. Finally, in Los Angeles, the group decided against accepting a Rolling Stones invitation to open a couple of shows for them, but they did pull a celebrity-packed audience to their first LA Roxy concert, including the aforementioned Stones, a couple of ex-Beatles, black stars Billy Preston and Buddy Miles, and Bob's Island label-mate Cat Stevens.

The measure of the Wailers' success across the US was that, during the tour, the Natty Dread album entered the American chart – their first chart success anywhere outside Jamaica. It gradually crept up to a

By the mid-Seventies Bob Marley and his music had become part of the mainstream of popular music, almost single-handedly establishing reggae as part of the rock scene generally

modest No.92, but was to remain a steady seller until the end of the year, remaining on the chart for a total of 28 weeks in all. Moreover, as the group began to get notably more American radio play (albeit on white rock stations rather than R&B outlets) during and after their tour, the sales of the previous two albums were also stimulated to modest chart-sized proportions: Burnin' reached No.151 in October, and Catch A Fire No.171 a month later.

In mid-July, flushed with their US progress, the group flew to Britain for a much shorter tour (just four dates), but at larger venues. Manchester and Birmingham hosted a concert apiece, and there were shows on two consecutive nights at London's Lyceum, the second of which Chris Blackwell recorded for a projected live album. Audience

Stevie Wonder was influenced by various music forms originating from elsewhere than his native USA, not least reggae

participation was total; Blackwell knew as his tapes rolled and as Bob rocked, preached and mesmerised from the stage that he finally had an international star on his hands.

When the UK tour wrapped, Bob flew back to America to visit Cedella in Delaware, and to briefly unwind, getting some song ideas together for the next album. He returned to Jamaica in August, and initial studio sessions involving new material started almost immediately. A song Bob had finally pulled into shape after working at it for some months was War, most of the lyric of which – suggested to him by Skill Cole – was the text of a speech given by Emperor Haile Selassie in February 1968 at Stanford University in California on the subject of the need for racial equality before there could be any hope for an end to conflict around the world. Transmuted into a stirring, emotional anthem, the song would henceforth be one of the most powerful highlights of the Wailers' stage show. Almost as soon as Bob had finally completed the song, however, on August 27 and at the age of 83, Emperor Haile Selassie died.

The Rastafarian faith shuddered, but it did not break. Selassie's death would make no difference in the long run to the strongly-rooted single-mindedness of the philosophy and way of life that his existence had initiated. Most Rastas simply did not believe in their leader's death, anyway: it stood to reason – as Bob Marley himself was heard to say – that you can't kill God.

Bob's immediate response, within days of the news, was a song which seemed to come spontaneously into being, and almost recorded itself without the need for rehearsal or preparation. Jah Live was a deeply-felt personal affirmation of his continuing faith, but it had the power to reach out to others too, and when rush-released on Tuff Gong as a Jamaican single, it was an immediate success.

In October, Bob finally had his first hit single outside Jamaica, too. Struck by the anthemic power and audience rapport of the version of No Woman, No Cry he had taped at the Lyceum, Chris Blackwell released the track as a UK single in advance of the planned album. He was gratified by strong airplay and a rapid UK chart entry, which saw the single peak at No.22. It also had the effect of finally pulling the Natty Dread album into British chart contention; a five-week run saw the LP peak at a respectable No.41.

While they were riding in the UK charts, Bob & the Wailers played a prestigious benefit show, known as the Dream Concert, in Jamaica, with another visiting American from the Motown stable, Stevie Wonder. Probably more than any other first-rank black US entertainer of the time, Wonder still avidly absorbed new and exciting music from outside his own sphere, and he consequently had checked out the Wailers closely during their US tour in June. Therefore, when Don Taylor approached him with the idea of headlining a joint stadium concert, with profits to go to a Jamaican Salvation Army Institute for the Blind, he eagerly agreed. The show took place on October 11, with Peter Tosh and Bunny Livingston both joining in segments of the Wailers act – the final time the original vocal group ever performed together. It was a huge success, highlighted by the Wailers and Wonder and his band jamming together on I Shot The Sheriff after the conclusion of the latter's own set. Stevie Wonder had been the biggest pop star with Jamaican audiences for some years, and the Dream Concert underlined the fact that Bob Marley & the Wailers had now attained equal stature. Marley was an international success, and a national institution.

FAMILY & FRIENDS

After Bob returned from his first, mid-1960s, sojourn in America, he and Rita got seriously down to family life, particularly after the couple retreated to live for some time on Bob's grandfather's old farmland in St. Ann. Their first two children, Cedella and David (who was nicknamed 'Ziggy' from an early age – a name under which he has become a star in his own right) were born in the country, in 1967 and 1968 respectively, and grew up alongside Sharon, Rita's first daughter, whom Bob adopted. In the early '70s, two more children would be born to the marriage: Stephen (commonly known in the family as Stevie) and Stephanie. It would be these two boys and three girls who, after their father's death and inspired by his career, would perform to great commercial success as Ziggy Marley & the Melody Makers.

During Bob's 1971 stay in Sweden and England, Rita and the young family lived in Delaware with the Booker family, Rita returning to her former profession as a nurse, working in a Wilmington hospital. Bob moved them back to Jamaica with part of his share of the group's initial advance from Island, but Rita was not happy at the prospect of settling back into Kingston, so the couple planned a move to Bull Bay, the up-coast Rasta-dominated settlement to which Bunny Livingston had also retreated. Bob planned to move there after recording the Catch A Fire album, but as soon as he became smitten by Island House at 56 Hope Road, Rita realised that his preferred base was not going to be hers. Consequently, in an archetypally Jamaican arrangement, just she and the children went to Bull Bay, and she remodelled much of the new family home herself: a therapeutic occupation when Bob was away overseas on the Catch A Fire tour.

Bob's Jamaican existence became somewhat hippyish, with much communal living (generally at Hope Road) which caught an echo of the Trench Town yard-dossing years in its looseness and cameraderie,

Top: Marley's son Damian photographed at their Jamaica home 'Island' in March 1980
Centre: Bob Marley was the toast of the rock 'n' roll establishment, particularly the Rolling Stones; here he relaxes with Mick Jagger
Bottom: Rita Marley
Opposite: Bob in 1980, already diagnosed as suffering from cancer, at 'Island House' with his wife Cindy Breakspeare

though with the benefit of comparative luxury, creative freedom and relative security of tenure. He would alternate this with spells at Bull Bay with Rita and the family, allowing him to keep a paternal eye on the children with the option of putting them at arm's length if either recording or performing dictated, or he felt the need to be the chief gypsy-in-residence at Hope Road.

This arrangement with Rita, above all, gave Bob the luxury of the space to follow his heart with regard to other women – a pursuit he never attempted to deny or play down, probably because it was almost an accepted social more among parts of Jamaica's population, and thus accepted by Rita as a fact of life.

Bob's romantic liaisons varied from brief on-tour assignations to lengthy affairs, and as his fame grew, these relationships began to involve women of increasingly celebrated status. There is no evidence that Bob particularly set out to deliberately enlarge his family with the aid of additional mothers, but his Rastafarian contempt for the unholy procedure of birth control, together with the fact that several of his paramours actively wanted to bear Bob Marley's child, meant that inevitably several of his relationships provided additions to his offspring.

In all, Bob had seven children outside his marriage, in addition to the four born to (and one adopted by) himself and Rita. Oldest of the additional clan was Robbie, whose mother was Pat Williams, an early member of the extended Hope Road 'commune'. Next came Rohan, born to another Kingston girlfriend named Janet, who appears to have departed the scene early on because her child was later adopted by Cedella, Bob's mother. A daughter, Karen, was conceived during Bob's 1971 UK stay, her English mother also being named Janet. Another English girlfriend gave birth to Julian in 1974 as the result of a tour liaison, while in the following year Bob's celebrity dalliance with Anita Bellnavis, the Caribbean women's table tennis champion, provided a daughter named Kimane.

Bob's most famous paramour of all, between 1975 and 1977, was Cindy Breakspeare, a young gymnast and PE instructor whose beauty also took her to the title of Miss Jamaica and, eventually, at the contest held in London in November 1976, to that of Miss World. After spending a holiday with Bob in the Bahamas over Christmas of that year, she gave birth to Damian Marley in 1977, while the final Marley offspring, born in 1979, was Makeba Janesta, the daughter of Yvette Morris, a long-time employee at 56 Hope Road.

A long-running celebrity liaison which did not provide a child was that between Bob and the Jamaican actress Esther Anderson, another of the regular Hope Road residents, which lasted through much of the early 1970s.

the Wailers' bassist, Family Man Barrett, who was his musical alter-ego through most of the band's Island recording career, sharing the production, arrangement and studio mixing duties. Bob's closeness to Family Man and Carlie Barrett on matters musical was such that there were periods during which other, newer members of the band would feel like outsiders to an élite clique, but the relationship was based on an almost symbiotic understanding of what made the Wailers' music tick, rather than any perceived two-tier grade of membership. Musicians were loyal to Bob because of the inspirational effect he had upon them: Wailers who, for reasons of their own, left the band to play elsewhere, tended to find an eventual magnetic pull back to the ranks – this happened with Earl Lindo, Al Anderson and Tyrone Downie.

The woman to whom Bob was closest during his years of fame, with the exception of his wife, mother, and – for intermittent periods – those with whom he was romantically involved, was Diane Jobson, his personal lawyer. An intelligent and well-educated Kingston woman, who by sheer coincidence had grown up in Kingston knowing the two sons of Robert Marley, (Norval Marley's brother, after whom he had named his own son), Diane was one of Bob's closest confidantes, and though she never actually took on the duties of manager, believing that a knowledge of the machinations of the music industry – which she didn't have – were a prerequisite for that role, her advice on business and financial matters generally, was something that Bob valued above many of his friendships.

For most of his adult life, when he was not writing, recording or performing music, sleeping, eating, drinking, making love or smoking herb, Bob Marley would be kicking a football around. Soccer was an almost addictive activity with him: his football skills had helped raise his currency in the ghetto, and it is quite feasible that in another time and place, in a society and culture without the elements so particular to Jamaica, Bob might have become a professional footballer. In real life, this was never on the agenda, but Bob became close friends with a man who had managed to take exactly that route, in the shape of Alan Cole, better known as 'Skill' because of his soccer prowess. Love of the game first brought the two men together, but they proved to be kindred spirits, sharing growing Rastafarian inclinations. Skill undertook organisational and occasional heavy muscle duties for Bob, and also became his general fitness guru, developing soccer kick-abouts into gruelling training workouts, and daily jogs into marathon fitness runs which, combined with the strict Rasta health food regime, helped kit out Bob and the Wailers for the rigours of international touring. It was into Skill Cole's arms that Bob would eventually collapse in 1980 after the stroke which signalled his terminal illness.

Perhaps the notable thing about all this extra-curricular family-making was that Bob acknowledged and supported all the children he knew to be his. Without exception, their mothers gave them the Marley surname on birth, and they grew up, and were educated and provided for, alongside Bob's 'official' offspring.

Bob's mother, so frequently parted from him during his childhood and adolescence, was probably the person to whom he was the closest during his adult life. Particularly once he gained the mobility of the celebrity traveller, the fact that she lived in the US was no barrier to frequent contact, and Cedella saw her grandchildren – all of them – on a regular basis. Her husband Edward died in February 1976, and once Cedella became a widow, Bob took a paternal interest in her welfare, eventually moving her to Miami where the climate was kinder and her grandchildren in closer proximity. Her closeness to Bob also resulted in Ciddy's eventual embrace of his Rastafarian faith, after decades as a fundamentalist Christian, while it was in deference to his mother that Bob was baptised into the Ethiopian Orthodox Church – as all his children had been – shortly before he died. Significantly, Cedella spent much time with him during Bob's final convalescent months, and she was the last person to whom he spoke before he died.

Many musicians and co-workers stayed almost literally by Bob's side for most of his working life, like Lee Jaffe, sometime Wailers harmonica player, Neville Garrick, Tuff Gong's design supremo, and most notably

VOTES & VIOLENCE

In 1962, the year in which Bob Marley cut his first single as a teenager, Jamaica was granted independence from Britain after three hundred years of colonial rule. Elsewhere in the world, such a rebirth of a nation might catalyse a new dynamism in domestic affairs, as the beneficiaries of independence set about internal reform and revitalisation – of the economy, the industrial base, and where necessary, of social inequities. In Jamaica, any such reforming zeal was apparently the baby that went out with the imperial bathwater, for the granting of independence turned out to be largely symbolic. In practical terms, very little changed: independent Jamaica remained an inert economy, an inadequate employer, and a land of social inequity where virtually all advantage, privilege and wealth devolved to essentially the same small minority which had held sway in former colonial days. For the majority of the population, poverty, hand-in-hand with repression, was the norm.

Government for most of the first decade after independence was by the JLP, the Jamaican Labour Party, which was widely perceived to be running the country for the benefit of the establishment: the neo-colonialist middle class. Coming from outside this privileged stratum of society, and identifying themselves in their music with the ghetto sufferers from whose ranks they had painfully hoisted themselves, the Wailers were traditionally considered a part of the liberal protest movement against this iniquitous status quo. The association was more by default than anything else: Marley or Wailers songs might sloganise on behalf of the underprivileged, but Bob and the group pointedly refused to throw their support behind any political grouping – and for a good, practical reason: political affiliation at ghetto street level in Jamaica tended to mean armed thugs and violent gangs, claiming allegiance to one side or other of the political divide, who took on their opposite numbers in savage street warfare. To side with any ghetto faction

Previous page, bottom: Bob Marley performing in 1976 just days after the failed attempt on his life by a politically motivated gunman which took place at his home in Hope Road
This page: Marley (pictured top at 'Island House') in March 1980 was considered a local and national hero by politicians, police and the ordinary community alike

effectively meant setting yourself up as a target for the other side, and the Wailers had too high a public visibility to risk becoming practice targets. Bob Marley would claim only to be on the side of the innocent victim, and there were plenty of those in the streets of Kingston.

A brief exception to the rule of neutrality came in 1971, when Bob became interested in the socialist rallying call of Michael Manley, the leader of the main opposition party, the PNP (People's National Party). Manley, a former union organiser, was the son of Norman Manley, who had been prime minister of the government 10 years earlier which had negotiated Jamaica's independence. With a general election due in 1972, Manley sensed the whiff of potential socialist revolution stirring among Jamaica's suffering classes. He began a long, nationwide campaign on a platform of righting social inequality, and attracted many younger people like Bob and Rita Marley to his rhetoric, while Manley in turn claimed that reggae music of the protesting and self-determining type (the Wailers' Trench Town Rock was a hit in Jamaica at the time) played an enlightening role in pinpointing for him, a non-ghetto dweller, the concerns and feeling of the people he was trying to reach with his own message. On a fairly casual basis, Bob joined Manley's travelling campaign for a while, performing as a solo singer/guitarist and helping articulate a voice of protest. He only stuck at it for a couple of weeks, however, before he and the Wailers flew off on the Autumn 1991 trip to the UK. When he eventually returned to Jamaica with the deal from Chris Blackwell under his belt, Bob had more immediate things to think about than political affiliation, and he was never again to willingly show any. Nevertheless, the wind of political change did blow, and when the elections were held in 1972, the PNP had a landslide victory which swept Michael Manley to power as Prime Minister.

By 1976, when Bob had risen to the status of an international star, another Jamaican election was in the offing. It was, inevitably, going to be another bitter struggle, if only because four years of PNP government had found Jamaica's deeply rooted social and economic problems impervious to a quick fix of socialism. Little had improved for the average citizen who had voted the party into power, while politically motivated violence now had a higher profile in the country than ever. In many ways, the Wailers' music over the intervening period had been both a mirror of this bleak political landscape and a rallying cry for a more revolutionary sweeping away of the world's iniquities. Nevertheless, Bob stayed well clear of the swirling political eddies, trying to keep his associations with the politicians' gun-toting henchmen from the ghetto, some of whom were friends from his adolescence, to a minimum – or, at the very least, fairly balanced between known PNP and JLP activists.

In any case, the Wailers had a more immediate agenda to attend to. The live album recorded in London was released at the tail-end of 1975 and reached No.38 on the UK chart, a peak five places higher than its predecessor. Musically, however, Live had only been a stop-gap, and the priority in the spring of 1976 was the completion of the studio album to be titled Rastaman Vibration, following which an international promotional tour would need to be planned. As Kingston suffered serious ghetto riots and a subsequent curfew during January, Bob and the band were battened down in Harry J's studio, completing the album.

Some new faces were around for these recording sessions, since both the Wailers' American players, Al Anderson and Lee Jaffe, had dropped out of the band following the last tour and were currently working instead with Peter Tosh on his own upcoming album project (released as Legalise It). Session player Earl 'Chinna' Smith, a longtime studio compadre of the band, filled in with basic guitar parts, while a new lead solo guitarist was found in the shape of Don Kinsey, another American blues/rock player with whom the Wailers had become acquainted on the previous year's US tour.

Bob during the 1978 'One Love' Peace Concert with Jamaican Labour Party leader Edward Seaga

The album, highlighted by the anthemic Haile Selassie speech adaptation War – the text of which had virtually become Bob's gospel of late during his discussions with interviewing journalists from the international media – was released in May 1976 and quickly became the Wailers' biggest-selling record yet, particularly in the US where, during the tour which followed its release, it was to become a top 10 hit, peaking at No.8 (in Britain it reached No.15 during a three-month chart residence). Another song included on the set was Rat Race, in which Bob voiced his anger over the current Jamaican political scene, and gave an overt warning to the warring factions that they were to leave him alone. 'Rasta,' proclaimed the songs, 'don't work for no CIA.' (The agency was rumoured to have a covert hand in some potentially destabilising JLP activities at this time.)

Rat Race was issued as a single in Jamaica, where it proved too confrontational to avoid a radio ban, but was a big street corner and sound system favourite. In the US, by contrast, the lyrically innocuous Rock, Roots, Reggae gave Bob his only substantial contact with the top 100 pop chart, reaching No.51 during the Wailers' US tour.

Through June, July and August, Bob Marley & the Wailers toured outside Jamaica again, playing their biggest shows in some of the largest venues they had yet aspired to. Initially, the tour went up and down the USA, from Miami to Philadelphia, through the major cities of the north-east and the mid-west, and then down the West Coast to California. Continental Europe was next, with dates in Germany, Holland, Belgium and France, and then the band toured the UK, where they played to their most passionate and energetic British audiences yet.

When the weary travellers returned to Jamaica during September, it was into a virtual state of emergency, with street violence at its worst level ever. Bob began to despair over what his country seemed bent

In Ambush In the Night Bob recalled the assasination attempt: 'See them fighting for power / But they know not the hour ... '

upon doing to itself. About the only thing that ever seemed to unite the gunmen, normally at each other's throats in the ghetto, was music, and notably the music of Bob Marley & the Wailers, which was fast finding a niche as a cornerstone of Jamaica's modern cultural heritage. This fact, a possible ray of hope, was not lost upon Bob, and in consultation with the Ministry of Culture, he proposed a sequel to the concert which the Wailers had played with Stevie Wonder at the end of the previous year, a show which would be the band's expression of thanks to the Jamaican audience for its long-term support, and would also place an emphasis on working for peace, and on the positive aspects of Jamaican life which lay beyond the gun battles.

The offer was readily accepted – too readily, as fairly soon became apparent. Shortly after the concert – dubbed Smile Jamaica after a new, upbeat song of that title which Bob had written to summarise the theme of the event – was announced for December 5 at the outdoor National Heroes Circle, the government made an announcement of its own that the general election would be held shortly afterwards, on December 15. All of a sudden, Smile Jamaica began to look like a PNP campaign junket, and Bob was, to say the least, not best pleased that the peace gesture had suddenly been cast in an overtly political light.

Preparations and rehearsals for the gig went ahead, but throughout November tangibly threatening vibes began to surround the whole project. An uninvited guard of PNP activists arrived to maintain a frequent security presence at 56 Hope Road, where the telephone would occasionally ring and an anonymous voice suggest that the event should not go ahead. Band rehearsals became tense as various musicians revealed themselves to be jittery about the situation. The I-Threes in particular were full of trepidation; Rita would regularly try to talk Bob out of it, while Judy was constantly feeling ill – the combined result of extreme nervousness and the fact that she was also pregnant. Marcia confronted Bob and said that if he insisted on the concert being played, she would not take part. Bob called her bluff, but she turned out to be serious – at the end of November, Marcia booked a plane ticket and left the island. He resigned himself to singing harmony with the I-Twos.

On the evening of December 3, the tension finally cracked: an event occurred which not only almost put paid to Smile Jamaica, but very nearly to Bob Marley as well, and was destined to change his life irrevocably. 56 Hope Road was just settling into an accustomed evening of rehearsal combined with relaxation as darkness fell. Judy Mowatt, however, was feeling violently ill, so Bob deputised art director Neville Garrick to take her home in Bob's car. As Garrick left the grounds of the house, manager Don Taylor drove his car in. Without anyone being aware of it, two more cars shadowed Taylor's entrance, and with the advantage of complete surprise, they suddenly disgorged themselves of six heavily armed men. Two stood guard in the yard, two started firing shots through Hope Road's windows, and two ran after Taylor into the house. Within seconds, one was firing randomly into the rehearsal room (blindly, his eyes clamped shut in terror, according to Tyrone Downie's girlfriend, who was trying to make herself invisible virtually next to him), while the other pursued Taylor into the kitchen, where Bob

Marley and guitarist Don Kinsey sat, having ducked out of rehearsal to take a grapefruit snack. This gunman apparently had his eyes open, but if Bob Marley was his intended target, Don Taylor was in his way. Of the seven or eight shots of automatic fire that the intruder got off before fleeing, five hit Don Taylor in the back of his legs and lower body, a couple went nowhere, and the last found Bob as Taylor went down in front of him; it grazed his chest and, more severely, his left arm. Outside, one of the men left near the car took aim at Rita, as she ran from a rear door surrounded by the Marley children. The single shot was a graze to her head, but it left a bullet fragment in her scalp and knocked her unconscious to the ground.

The gunmen dashed for their cars and went out of the gates and down the street at high speed, probably panicked by the siren of an approaching police car which had ben alerted by the sounds of gunfire. After a couple of frozen, silent minutes, the arrival of the police brought the unwounded out of their hiding places. Bob and the semi-conscious Rita were bundled into a car which raced to University College Hospital, while an ambulance was called for Don Taylor, who was losing blood heavily, and a Wailers friend named Lewis Griffith, who had been hit in

'... Ambush in the night, they opened fire on me
Ambush in the night, protected by His Majesty ...'

the stomach by one of the bullets fired through a window. There were no other injuries, but nobody was going to stay around and tempt fate. As soon as the ambulance left, the musicians and their friends made themselves scarce, and 56 Hope Road was left empty under heavy police guard.

Prime Minister Manley went to the hospital as soon as the news reached him, and set an instant security operation into motion. Bob's wounds were comparatively minor, needing some treatment and bandaging. Rita was in a hospital bed, also bandaged, but conscious and relatively comfortable. Griffith needed surgery, and Taylor was on the critical list as he was rushed to theatre. (Against the odds, he would survive and make a full recovery.)

In the small hours of the morning, the Jamaican security service quietly removed Bob from the hospital and drove him up into the hills above Kingston to a secluded house named Strawberry Hill, owned by Chris Blackwell and used by Bob as a secret retreat in the past. He spent a nervous, bewildered night there, an armed police detachment spread around the grounds, while Manley's security men brought those of Bob's regular entourage who had not dropped completely out of sight (like Family Man Barrett, who remained invisible for days) up into the mountains to join him. The Prime Minister was determined that the Smile Jamaica concert should go on despite this shock attack, but he was aware that Bob needed some space, time and security to regroup and consider his position.

If there had been debate about whether to go ahead with Smile Jamaica before, it was even more protracted now. Throughout Saturday December 4, the day before the concert was due, Bob and his closest friends tried, once the physical shock had departed, to come to terms with what had happened, who could have been responsible and – the

thought uppermost in many people's minds – whether it would happen again as soon as Bob Marley once more showed his face in public – from a concert stage, for instance. The fact that the would-be assassins were totally unknown was the most worrying thing, since without any knowledge of motive, it was impossible to judge whether this had been a one-off warning – nobody had, after all, been killed – or a bungled first attempt in what could be a concerted effort to remove Bob Marley, for whatever reason, from the picture.

Bob was happy enough to be removed, in the sense that on that Saturday he would gladly have gathered up wife and children and departed Jamaica on the first available flight. The decision to be made over the concert was what kept him in place, once the fear of immediate vulnerability had subsided. Bob's feeling was that the show was probably a no-no; after all, most of the Wailers were still in hiding, and there was no guarantee that they could be found in time.

During the day on Sunday December 5, Rita came out of hospital, bandaged about the head but otherwise in fair shape, and some of the band – Carlie Barrett, Tyrone Downie and Don Kinsey – regrouped at 56 Hope Road in order to find out what was happening. The Ministry of Culture had made no announcement of a cancellation, so during the afternoon, a large crowd began to assemble at the National Heroes Circle anyway, despite having heard the news of the shooting, which was splashed all over the local media. Peter Tosh, Bunny Livingston (or Bunny Wailer, as he now billed himself professionally) and Burning Spear were all scheduled to play in the earlier stages of the event, but all of them took valour's better part and failed to turn up. At Strawberry Hill, there was much argument and counter-argument going on; everyone knew the final decision would be Bob's, and it was basically a tustle between his friends (plus Rita) who wanted to let the concert go, and those with PNP connections, notably government minister Tony Spaulding, who were determined that the event should survive. Bob's mind was eventually made up both by Spaulding's eloquent persuasion, and by a phone call to his friend, bassist Cat Coore of the band Third World. Cat, whose band had just finished playing their allotted slot, assured Bob that the vibe was right; the audience, which now numbered thousands, was in a positive mood, and in palpable expectation of the Wailers' appearance. Cat also agreed to play bass, Family Man being the one key Wailer whom the police had been utterly unable to trace during the weekend.

The Marley shooting was not an entirely unique incident; Jamaican politics were fraught with violence during the Seventies

The high tension among political groups – many of them armed – was particularly evident at election time

The decision made, a motorcade with armed police protection raced down from the hills into Kingston, delivering Bob virtually to the stage of the arena, where Michael Manley was there to publicly greet him.

The pick-up Wailers, augmented by the Zap Pow Horns and Cat Coore in Family Man's place, assembled around him, with Rita (still in her hospital gown, since she had not been able to get access to any of her own clothes) and Judy Mowatt joining them. Bob began with a cry from the heart to the audience, telling them of his sadness that politics were now moulding this event which he had conceived as a tribute to peace and to the people of Jamaica. For the people, Bob said, he would play one song while he was here and, guitarless (his left arm was too sore to play), he went straight into a passionate War. During this, the fire of performance took hold, and the band continued to play some of their best-known anthems: Trench Town Rock, Rastaman Vibration and others, in a driven musical segue lasting almost 90 minutes. Bob closed by showing his two bullet scars to the audience and, with a dramatic laugh of defiance, mimed a gunfighter firing back at imaginary assailants. With that, as the crowd applauded deliriously, he was gone, spirited away once again by the security forces to his secluded hideout.

The next morning, still not knowing whether he was a target for an unknown assassin, Bob quietly left Jamaica, accompanied by Neville Garrick, on a private plane which Chris Blackwell had hastily chartered. Their destination, initially at least, was Blackwell's Caribbean headquarters in Nassau, the Bahamas, where it was planned that Bob's family and the Wailers would join him within days.

The Jamaican elections took place as scheduled, a week or so later, resulting in another heavy PNP win, while Bob Marley, whether or not he had been regarded as a factor in the fortunes of one side or the other, was far removed from the politics that he had tried, in any case, to avoid with all his might. The shooting had achieved that, and some speculated that perhaps that was all it had been meant to achieve. For Bob, it meant a year in which he actually feared to return to his homeland; he was a superstar in exile on the World stage. It was the time of Exodus.

BABYLON BECKONS

Bob and the Wailers spent the first half of 1977 in London. The immediate concern was the preparation and recording of a new album, so over a period of some weeks, staying in a comfortable communal Chelsea flat with the band, Bob, with his mind freed by distance from the unanswered questions over the shooting, was able to work on completing many songs which had been left unfinished in Jamaica, and developing some new ones which had been spurred by the events of late 1976. By the time rehearsals transferred to Island's studios in Basing Street, over 20 songs were near completion, and the sessions would actually produce enough material not only for the next album Exodus, but its follow-up Kaya 12 months later. The Wailers also

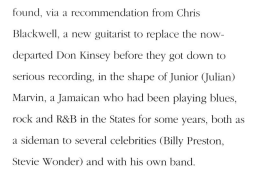

found, via a recommendation from Chris Blackwell, a new guitarist to replace the now-departed Don Kinsey before they got down to serious recording, in the shape of Junior (Julian) Marvin, a Jamaican who had been playing blues, rock and R&B in the States for some years, both as a sideman to several celebrities (Billy Preston, Stevie Wonder) and with his own band.

During the weeks of recording, Bob was invited by the Ethiopian Orthodox Church in London to meet their exiled Crown Prince Asfa Wossan, who was the grandson of Haile Selassie. The meeting lasted a fruitful two hours, and it transpired that the Crown Prince was familiar with Marley and his music, while the somewhat over-awed Bob had plenty to ask about Ethiopia and the late Emperor. Before they parted, Wossan pre-sented him with a Lion of Judah ring which, he said, had belonged to Selassie. Bob was staggered that it closely resembled a ring he had worn in a still vividly remembered dream during his adoles-

cence, and henceforth treated the gift as his most treasured possession, wearing it continuously until his death.

The Exodus album was released in May 1977 and was highlighted by some of the most widely successful songs of Bob's career, like the

---

Marley on stage was a photographer's dream, as evidenced by the stun-ning work of David Corio (previous page, main picture) and Paul Slattery (opposite)
Other striking images came out of informal shots of Bob relaxing: this page, top, by Serge Assier, and bottom, caught in familiar smoking pose by Patrick Chauvel

---

anthemic title track, the party dancer Jammin', the Cindy Breakspeare-inspired Waiting In Vain and the medley of the Wailers' own oldie One Love with Curtis Mayfield's 1960s spiritual People Get Ready, as well as more personal numbers like Natural Mystic and the topical Guiltiness and So Much Things To Say, both of which had grown out of anger over the attempted assassination. Just prior to the album's release, both Bob and Family Man were arrested and fined for marijuana possession in London – which finally alerted the British press to the fact that the Wailers were in the country – so they were probably relatively pleased to get out on the road shortly afterwards to commence the European/UK tour that had been organised to promote Exodus.

The tour opened in Paris where, during off-duty time devoted to the inevitable game of football against a tough-tackling team of French jour-nalists, a highly significant accident occurred. Bob's right big toe was crushed during a tackle, which sent him limping off the field. Despite first aid, including cutting off most of the smashed toenail, it proved impossible for the wound to heal up properly under the punishing con-ditions of life on the road and on stage. The tour swung on through Belgium, Holland, Germany and Scandinavia, before eventually coming back in June for a trek around Britain. All the while, Bob travelled and performed against a permanent background of pain from his foot.

When the tour returned to the UK, the Exodus album took off in the British charts, climbing as high as No.8 – the first UK top 10 placing achieved by a Bob Marley album. So consistent were sales to be over the longer term, that Exodus would finally exit the UK album chart more than 12 months later. Moreover, the title track found simultaneous release as a UK single, and this performed almost as well as the album, given impetus by the excitement generated from the tour, charting for two months and hitting an eventual high point of No.14 – the first UK top 20 entry by a Marley single.

When the UK tour ended, Bob took a two-week holiday at Cedella's house in Delaware, intending to rest before the US Exodus tour started in New York in July. Within days, though, he was back in London, con-sulting a foot specialist. By now, the stubbornly unhealed toe was dri-ving him to distraction: every night on tour he would finish up virtually limping offstage because of the pain from his right foot, aggravated by the spontaneous dancing with which his performance was peppered. Each night the damage to the toe would again manifest itself in a bloody, swollen, infected mess, and relaxing in Wilmington seemed to do nothing to help it, because after Bob had rested the foot, he would find he could hardly walk on it.

The London specialist made a close examination of the wound, infection, toe, and foot in general, and his conclusion after analysing the

test results was ominous – Bob's injury was not healing because the toe itself was effectively sick: examination under the microscope had revealed cancer cells. The doctor recommended that the entire toe be amputated as early as possible in order to check further spread of the cancerous cells.

The suggestion that he should lose part of his foot shocked Bob possibly even more than the news that he had cancer. Since the healing process following the suggested amputation would be comparatively rapid, it was unlikely to affect the planned US tour too badly, but the very fact that most of those around him immediately backed this course pushed Bob's own feelings further in the opposite direction. The specialist's alternative was a minor skin amputation, careful cleansing, and a much longer recuperation period, which was far more to Bob's liking even if it meant the cancellation of a vital tour. Pulled every which way, he sought a second opinion in Miami, visiting the surgeon who had saved the now virtually recovered Don Taylor's life after the shooting.

The diagnosis and the suggested treatment were the same: some of the injured toe, at least, would have to go.

While Bob was under the knife at the Cedars of Lebanon hospital in Miami, an announcement was made to the world in general that the Wailers' US tour was to be postponed, possibly until 1978. The stated reason, which glossed over the truth about as far as it was possible to without fabricating some other illness, was that Bob needed treatment for an injury sustained while playing football.

Bob had been pursuing plans to move Cedella and her family to the warmer climate of Florida for some time. Now, when he came out of hospital, making what seemed to be quite a rapid recovery, the house he had bought in Vista Lane, Miami, proved an ideal place to recuperate, surrounded by close family and friends. Meanwhile, although bereft of its anticipated live promotion, the Exodus album sold well across the US, mainly due to wide radio airplay on both white and black-orientated stations. It eventually pulled up at No.20 on the American album chart, not quite equalling the impact of Rastaman Vibration, but proving enough of a success – as it had all around the world – to re-enthuse the convalescent Bob who, as he literally regained his feet, began to write songs once again. He also had the overdubbing and remixing of the second batch of London 1977 recordings moved to Miami's Criteria Studio, so that he would be on hand to supervise it.

Back in the UK, where Exodus continued as a bestseller, Bob Marley & the Wailers were becoming regular visitors to the singles chart, too. At least part of the reason was that much of the punk audience which emerged from the working-class woodwork in Britain around this time, focusing on the mixture of nihilism, protest and rejection of musical virtuosity as personified by the Sex Pistols, the Clash, the Damned and a

sudden heaving sea of other punk bands, also rated reggae very highly. Jamaican records would have their most commercially successful period in the UK since the first flush of reggae hits in 1969/70, over the three years from mid-1977 – and the Wailers, who had both an existing high profile and a militant outsider image with which punk youth could readily identify, were the first act to benefit. The second single from Exodus, Waiting In Vain, reached No.27 in the UK chart in September, while the third, the dance-friendly Jammin', hit No.9 at the end of the year – Bob's first British top 10 single. Its success was also down to its double A-side coupling – a track which Bob had recorded (aided in the studio by members of Third World and the British reggae act Aswad) in London early in the year when Lee Scratch Perry had been in town. Based upon Scratch's observations of London punkhood, Punky Reggae Party paid tribute to this strange new audience's eagerness for Jamaican music – there were probably as many buying it for the topical Perry collaboration as for Jammin'.

As 1978 dawned, Don Taylor, now himself fully recovered from the shooting incident, began to plan a Wailers world tour. Based around the recently completed Kaya album, this would open in the US in May as, effectively, the replacement for the postponed Exodus trek, before covering Europe in the summer, and eventually Australia, New Zealand and Japan during the autumn.

One place the tour was not, initially, planned to take in was Jamaica. Bob had no intention of returning home while he felt his life could still be in danger, and since the would-be assassins had never officially been identified or apprehended (there were plenty of rumours, like the gunmen having been murdered by those who had hired them, to ensure their silence), he had no reason to believe that they would not try to

This page: Bob Marley shot by top UK photographer Jill Furmanowsky during his world tour of 1978

At home in 1980: Bob Marley visibly deteriorated as his cancer became more evident with the the passing months

strike again. However, an unusual set of circumstances was to alter this decision.

With Jamaica almost in a state of self-destruction, thanks to unchecked violent crime and politically-motivated infighting, the PNP government had put the country under virtual martial law during 1977. The police were now pursuing a policy of arresting and jailing known 'faces' simply for being who they were, while the army was taking on the street gangs, and the latter were dying wholesale, faced with infinitely superior firepower.

In January 1978, against this desperate background, the Jamaica Peace Movement came into being, sponsored by the Rastafarian sect known as the Twelve Tribes of Israel, with which Bob was known to be sympathetic. Bob's involvment with the peace movement, which prefaced eventual deep involvement in the Twelve Tribes too, was initiated, ironically, by two leading members of the warring gang elements. Politically-affiliated street toughs Claudie Massop (JLP) and Bucky Marshall (PNP) had both known Bob since teenage days on the Trench Town streets. Though they were enemies by political persuasion, when they were jailed together and found that Marley was a common factor in their lives, they came up with the idea that if a truce on the streets could be agreed on the basis of Bob coming back to Jamaica to play a symbolic concert for peace and unity as part of the Twelve Tribes initiative, the warfare might cease (the losing war against the army, that is) before they and their urban guerrilla armies were all dead.

Bob was advised of these proposals during a visit to him in Miami by Vernon Carrington, or Prophet Gad, the Twelve Tribes of Israel leader, who also accepted Bob into the sect under the new name of Joseph (Twelve Tribes doctrine involved identification with the Biblical twelve sons of Jacob, seeing the black race as descendents of the lost tribe of Israel, sold into Babylonian captivity from which it now sought redemption). Sceptical of Claudie Massop's motives because he assumed Massop had been close to his would-be assassins, Bob agreed only to meet him on distant neutral ground in London. However, with PNP-affiliated gunman Tony Welch also in attendence to demonstrate the truce, and with Massop guaranteeing Bob's safety in Jamaica from the JLP elements which had (it was now admitted) wanted Bob off the scene during the last election, he agreed to ally himself with the Peace Movement and to play a showcase performance which would be symbolic of that movement's unifying goal, as well as having a practical purpose in rasing money for specific projects in rundown West Kingston. From its timing, the event could also act as the springboard for the Wailers' world tour, which would be dedicated to harmony and love – the dominant themes on the Kaya album. In press conferences prior to going back to Jamaica, Bob continually stressed his own neutral stance politically as well as his commitment to the unity of spirit, particularly among the black race, which was a key element in the Rastafarian faith and also the essential basis of the Peace Movement.

Bob eventually returned to Kingston and 56 Hope Road from his
15-month exile in March 1978. He immediately began to rehearse the
Wailers for the Peace Concert, scheduled for April 22. It would be their
first live gig since early the previous summer, and Bob was determined
to get the band into ultra-tight shape again, both for this show and the
massive tour to follow. Al Anderson rejoined the line-up to create a twin
guitar lead with the now firmly entrenched Junior Marvin while, after an
even longer hiatus, Wire Lindo also came back into the fold to double
up the keyboards strength with Tyrone Downie.

At the end of the month, Kaya was released worldwide, startling
those who expected more righteous militancy with its laid-back paeans
to love, herb (Kaya being a Rasta term for ganga), dancing, and general
spiritual and bodily refreshment. In the UK, it zoomed straight up to
No.4, Bob's highest chart position yet, while the extracted single Is This
Love equalled Jammin' by reaching No.9. The album began to climb the
US charts too, though it peaked a couple of months later at a rather
more muted No.50.

The One Love Peace Concert took place on Saturday, April 22, amid
an almost supernatural high of expectation from the Jamaican population, and a vast police security operation which extended from the
venue, Kingston's National Stadium, back to the now securely-patrolled
gates of 56 Hope Road. As the breathless truce reigned in the shanty
towns, a capacity crowd filled the stadium, including Prime Minister
Michael Manley, JLP Opposition leader Edward Seaga, and a host of
senior politicians and officials from both their parties. Of all the many
acts currently popular on the Jamaican recording scene, only Bob's former Wailers partner Bunny declined to attend, out of scepticism over
the whole notion of the peace movement. A dozen or so other acts
played through the afternoon, leading up to an appearance by Peter
Tosh which galvanised much of the audience and enraged the high-
rankers when Tosh lectured them – Manley and Seaga by name –
between songs with a catalogue of Jamaica's social iniquities. The fact
that he ostentatiously lit up a spliff of ganga as he did his haranguing
certainly did not endear Tosh to the assembled officialdom, but with a
vast popular vote clearly going for him from the massed ranks behind
the VIP seats, Peter judged himself – rightly – safe from any police move

which might have sparked a riot. (He was closely watched after the concert, however, and when police finally spotted him a few months later with another spliff in his hand in public, he was busted and severely beaten, as Kingston's offended police took their revenge.)

For most of the 30,000 audience, however, the raison d'être of the concert was Bob Marley & the Wailers, and the tightly-rehearsed band,

suspicion – had hidden agendas behind the approach which brought Bob Marley back to his homeland, time was not allowed to tell. Violent confrontation had not vanished from the world they inhabited: Massop was shot dead early in 1979 and Marshall likewise during 1980.

The 1978 world tour proper opened in Cleveland, Ohio, on May 19, with the Wailers in their most dynamic, professional and hard-driven

adrenalised by the sense of occasion, did not disappoint. The songs were familiar and the performances, from the opening Trench Town Rock to War, were triumphal. The penultimate number was the symbolically unifying anthem One Love, midway through which Bob, in a manner which made him seem the mouthpiece of most of those present in the stadium, requested Michael Manley and Edward Seaga to join him on stage in a mutual public show of support for the Peace Movement. By the time the two political adversaries were flanking him as the Wailers pushed One Love to a climax, Bob, his eyes closed, seemed almost transcendent. Grasping both politicians' hands, he hoisted their arms aloft in his own, creating a tableau of unlikely unity which forever stands as the key visual image of that concert.

If the One Love concert did not bring rapid, lasting peace to the Kingston streets, it made its mark as a significant event in post-colonial Jamaican history, in which a wholly Jamaican self-help initiative achieved a stature – thanks to Bob Marley – which matched the dignity of its aspirations. As to whether Claudie Massop and Bucky Marshall – of whose motives in originally mooting the event there was widespread

Marley during his last world tour, including a shot at the Paris concerts (left) which were recorded for a live album

shape ever. For more than a month they criss-crossed between the cities of the eastern United States and Canada, selling out everywhere, including the vast Madison Square Garden venue in New York. The Big Apple was also the venue for a moving presentation to Bob of the Third World Peace Medal – a presentation sponsored by the African delegations to the United Nations in honour of his globally-heard musical pleas for justice and equality.

Late June and early July saw European dates in France, Spain, Sweden, Denmark, Norway, Holland, Belgium and the UK, where another single from Kaya, Satisfy My Soul, rode the top 30 on the back of the Wailers' concerts. The Paris shows from this trek were recorded by Island to form the basis of the year-end double live album release, Babylon By Bus.

Late in July, the tour returned to North America, playing down the West Coast from Vancouver in Canada to California. At the Burbank concert, Peter Tosh joined Bob onstage for the first time in years during Get Up, Stand Up, a song which they had co-written.

The final part of the world tour, after a short hiatus in Jamaica, took Bob and the Wailers for the first time to the Far East and Pacific rim. The fact that the band had never toured this region before only heightened audience expectation and response: the gigs in Japan, Australia and New Zealand were sold-out and ecstatic. After the traumas of violence in 1976, and the health scare of 1977, 1978 was a triumphal year. It also closed on a personal high note for Bob as he finally made a long-hoped-for visit to Africa and, in particular, Ethiopia where he made a fruitful stay in Addis Ababa (along with Skill Cole who, also a long-term absentee from Jamaica after the December 1976 shooting, was now semi-resident in the country coaching a major Ethiopian football team). While the chief reason for Bob's visit was to experience at first hand the cradle of his Rastafarian faith, and to visit everything he could that was associated with Haile Selassie, his very presence on African soil enabled him to soak up at first hand the issues currently preoccupying native Africans. Chief among these was the guerrilla war in the illegally independent, minority-ruled ex-British colony of Rhodesia, where the Ethiopian government was overtly supporting the nationalist Patriotic Front armies of Robert Mgabe and Joshua Nknomo. From a comparatively close-view study of this conflict, Bob wrote, while he was staying in Addis Ababa, the song Zimbabwe – after the name by which the guerrilla fighters called their country – as a tribute to what he saw as an historic struggle against oppression.

Bob returned to Jamaica at the beginning of 1979 to a new recording environment: the state-of-the-art Tuff Gong recording studio at 56 Hope Road, which had been built and equipped under chief executive Diane

Jobson's supervision during the Wailers' lengthy absence on tour. The first part of the year was mostly spent there, with Bob completing, honing and recording the first major body of songs since that in 1977 which had produced both the Exodus and Kaya albums. The working title for the new album was Black Survival, reflective of the fact that much of Bob's recent material was heavily political and frequently dark in tone – reflections of his African experience, the deteriorated situation in Jamaica following the failure of the Peace Movement to maintain its initial momentum, and Bob's own general state of mind, which many close to him in that period described as bleak, sometimes distracted, and often short-fused. Despite outward bodily health (he played soccer as energetically as ever), he was still on an ongoing programme of anti-cancer medication, and this too was thought to be a factor in his demeanour.

The album eventually appeared in October, with co-production by Alex Sadkin, as Survival, a release overtly dedicated to black solidarity in general, and the African struggle for self-determination in particular, through songs like Africa Unite, So Much Trouble In The World and Zimbabwe. Bob also exorcised a few more of the demons of the attempted assassination with Ambush In The Night, while the song Survival itself was a prophesy of Third World inheritance following the annihilation of the powers of Babylon.

The Wailers had played three major live shows earlier in the year: the Reggae Sunsplash festival in Montego Bay, Jamaica, and a fund-raising benefit concert for African freedom fighters at the Harvard University stadium in Boston, USA, during July, and another Kingston benefit show for local causes during September. The Survival tour itself began early in October with four nights at the symbolically historic showcase of American black music, the Apollo Theatre in Harlem, New York. These were followed by an arduous two-month trek around Canada and the USA, with a final date in December in Nassau, the Bahamas, which was a benefit for the United Nations International Year of the Child, a cause close to the heart for father-of-eleven Bob Marley. To it, he donated all royalties from his song Children Playing In The Streets, which had recently been released as a single by the Melody Makers, a vocal group made up of his and Rita's own children.

The Survival album, possibly due to its particular preoccupations, and possibly because the tour supporting it was confined to North America, did not prove to be quite as big a seller as Exodus or Kaya, globally. It reached No.20 in the UK and in the US peaked at a modest

Robert Mugabe, Prime Minister of Zimbabwe (formerly Rhodesia) whose Independence Day Marley helped celebrate in 1980

Bob signing autographs for fans at a Los Angeles branch of Tower Records in November 1979

No.70, notwithstanding the Wailers' high touring profile there. At the beginning of 1980 the whole band visited Africa, which led to an unexpected time of reckoning for manager Don Taylor. The Wailers were invited to Gabon to help celebrate the birthday of President Bongo, and played a couple of modest (in terms of audience size – those attending were all invited) concerts in the capital, Libreville. A minor query over the payment for their services, however, led to the sudden discovery by Bob and his lawyer Diane Jobson that Don Taylor had significantly raised Bob's comparatively nominal fee (he was pleased just to be in Africa again) with the clear intention of siphoning off a large amount for himself. Enraged by the disgrace he considered this irregularity to have brought upon him in the eyes of his Gabonai hosts, Bob allegedly rough-handled Taylor into admitting what he had done, in the course of which investigation it transpired that similar fee-hikings had been going on for years; Taylor had desperate gambling debts and had been paying them off with the portions of tour receipts his employer knew nothing about. Bob dismissed his manager forthwith, and the Wailers returned from Gabon to the UK, where the new album was to be recorded, in deeply depressed spirits.

All things considered, the sessions for the Uprising album at the Island studios went well, an abundance of strong material emerging from which the LP selections could be made. Bob then took some time off in Kingston (for his 35th birthday) and Florida. At his Miami home,

he conferred at length with old mentor (and still, to a large extent, his song publisher) Danny Sims. They spoke about Bob's management difficulties and also his recording future, since Island's contract with Tuff Gong would officially end with the release of Uprising. Sims announced that the international major company PolyGram Records was interested in signing the Wailers once Chris Blackwell's option ran out, and Bob asked Sims to pursue this possibility on his behalf.

Another invitation then arrived to play in Africa, on a basis far removed from the recent Gabon trip which had ended in such a débâcle. Its future finally decided by a new deal with Britain on legal independence and by the cessation of hostilities and victory at the ballot box for the Patriotic Front, Rhodesia was to emerge as the newly independent African republic of Zimbabwe on April 17, 1980. Bob Marley was invited to attend the Independence Ceremony as an official overseas dignitory, in recognition of the role that his music, and particularly the song Zimbabwe, had played in assisting the new nation's spiritual struggle towards self-determination. Moreover, the Wailers were invited to play a concert in Salisbury, the capital, as part of the official programme of celebrations. Bob regarded this as one of the greatest honours ever bestowed upon him, and replied that he would play for no fee, covering the Wailers' expenses himself (the cost to his pocket would eventually be estimated at $250,000, since the band flew in from London their stage

and new Uprising material, and the audiences were among the largest they had ever seen – 100,000 at the Crystal Palace Garden Party in London on June 6, a similar number in Dublin on July 6, and a staggering 180,000 in Milan on June 27. When the last date was completed and the band returned to London to rest in mid-July, Bob was haggard and exhausted, and in the minds of many, noticeably ill. He was fine when playing football (Skill Cole was back as a road manager, which meant that the Wailers' five-a-side team was virtually undefeatable), but otherwise he could easily lapse into distant distraction, and ate badly. Most tellingly, once he was offstage, the celebrated piercing look from the Marley eyes was dimmed.

The commercial success of the band, on the other hand, was anything but subdued. Bolstered by the wildly successful tour, Uprising sold hugely all over Europe, easily eclipsing the previous year's Survival. In the UK, the album peaked at No.6 in the chart, with the extracted hit single Could You Be Loved going one better at No.5, and its follow-up Three Little Birds also making the top 20.

While the Wailers returned to Jamaica to prepare for the second Tuff Gong Uprising tour around North America, Bob flew to Miami to rest at home and also meet again with Danny Sims to discuss PolyGram's recording interest. Sims confirmed that the multinational company was indeed interested in taking the Wailers on a multi-million dollar deal, but he also had a personal warning to pass on to Bob, which had indirectly come to him from CIA sources. Another Jamaican general election was near, and the CIA was determined that this time Edward Seaga's JLP party would oust Michael Manley's socialist PNP government. Bob Marley was an unknown factor which the agency did not want on the scene in Jamaica, whether he overtly resurrected ancient support for Manley or not. 'Remember what happened to Bob Marley and his family before the last election,' Sims' associate told him, 'and keep him out of the country.' Bob knew precisely what was meant; he stayed in Miami and brought the rest of his family there, as Kingston once more began its pre-election course of self-destruction. It was a prudent decision, made in reaction to the situation of the moment, but in fact it also meant that Bob was destined never to see Jamaica again. Though nobody knew it at the time – even though many of those close to him continued to worry about his health – by the summer of 1980, Bob Marley had already slowly begun to die.

gear, an entire PA system and even the customised stage on which they would play).

The Independence Ceremony, and the celebratory concert which followed it the next night at Rufaro Stadium, were triumphs for the Wailers. For Bob, it seemed a personal triumph of accomplishment to see the old colonial Union Jack lowered for the last time and handed to Prince Charles (ceremonially handing over independence as the Queen's representative), and the new flag of Zimbabwe hoisted in its place. In their concert performance, the Wailers were fired by the sense of history and occasion surrounding them, and the 40,000 audience responded in ecstatic kind.

In June, the new album Uprising was released, by which time the Wailers had already launched the Tuff Gong Uprising tour in Europe, which lasted from May 30 to July 13 – a punishing schedule, even allowing for jet (and some luxury bus) travel – and which would see 31 concerts in as many different cities, passing through twelve countries and performing to over a million people. The Wailers played long sets (up to three hours, including encores), packed with a balance of familiar hits

HIS MUSICAL WORD LIVES ON

DEPARTURE & LEGACY

The American Tuff Gong Uprising tour was scheduled to start on September 14 in Boston, and the Wailers regrouped in Miami during August to prepare for it, at which point all could see a physical change for the worse in Bob. Privately, various members of the entourage started worrying about the old cancer problem, even though this had supposedly been held in check after Bob's operation by medication and regular examinations. Bob even now had his personal doctor Carl Frazier as a permanent part of the touring retinue, and the doctor had voiced no worries publicly about the upcoming trek across the States, so everything had to be all right – yet Bob was obviously tired much of the time, and occasionally also complained that there was

something wrong with his voice. In a business sense, the tour was essential: although Uprising was indeed rising up the US chart, it was not yet repeating its European success (it would eventually peak at No.45, 25 places higher than the US peak of Survival), and the live shows were expected to boost sales much as the European trek had done.

The Boston opening date went well enough, although a close observer might have noted that Bob was tired well before the end of the show (which followed an earlier Wailers running order, decided at the last minute, rather than that of the three-hour European spectaculars), and that the rest of the band were somewhat subdued because they recognised the fact. The scenario was the same the next night in Providence, Rhode Island. A day later, on arrival in New York, where the Wailers would be playing two major shows at Madison Square Garden on successive evenings, opening for the top US Motown soul band, the Commodores, the band members – and even Rita and the I-Threes – were surprised to find themselves accommodated in a different hotel from Bob, with a couple of miles distance between. The reason given by the tour organisers, by road manager Alan Cole and by Dr Frazier, was

Previous page, top: Ziggy Marley
Previous page, main picture: Bob Marley's coffin during his State Funeral in Kingston
This page, top: A commemorative painting of Marley
Centre: Entrance to the Bob Marley Museum
Bottom: Commemorative statue of Marley

that Bob was in an exhausted state and needed time to sleep between shows without interruption. This explanation failed to convince anyone and when friends and musicians visited Bob at the Essex House hotel off Central Park, they found his suite abuzz with unknown hangers-on. Bob was isolated all right, resting behind the closed door of his bedroom, but such was the nervous disorganisation around him that a virtual circus had him besieged – why, then, were those who knew him best being kept at arm's length?

The first Madison Square Garden concert started badly for the group. Disorganisation during the afternoon had prevented a proper sound check, and it took a while before the Wailers even sounded like themselves, after they started playing in the evening. Bob had accepted the afternoon's escalating delays with uncommon weary stoicism – he was having to ride on a constantly refuelled herb high to stay alert to the business in hand; once it came to the actual performance, however, the natural high and ecstacy of his music took over, and the show was fiery and potent, somewhat to the band's relief. Another day of exhausted isolation followed, and then the second New York show also delivered the goods – although Bob was said to have had a moment of near-collapse, from which he managed to recover towards the end of his performance. An additional incentive which may have helped him through the evening was the appearance backstage of Danny Sims with PolyGram's president, offering a $10 million five-album deal, including a $3 million advance and PolyGram taking a worldwide release option on all Tuff Gong's other artists and product. The future could be commercially rosy. Bob's problem was that he could hardly get his bearings on the present any more. Following the Wailers' set, he again returned to Essex House in pain and total exhaustion.

On Sunday morning, September 21, Bob, after declining Rita's phone invitation to go to church (a local Ethiopian Orthodox service) with her because he had not slept sufficiently, decided to get some air and exercise. Alan Cole and Dr Frazier accompanied him on a jog in the adjacent park, and Skill was running by his side when Bob suddenly, nightmarishly, felt his neck seize up and his body 'freeze', as if somebody had jerked out a vital connecting plug. With total loss of control, he was only able to yell for Cole's help as he pitched into his arms. He remained conscious on the ground, but totally immobilised and unable to move his head. His badly shaken friends carried him back to the hotel suite, where feeling and movement slowly came back, but Dr Frazier recognised the signs of a stroke and immediately made arrangements to get Bob to a neurologist on Monday morning.

Rita and the band were told nothing of this, despite Rita's frequent phone calls later in the day to discover what was happening. Skill Cole would simply not let anybody, even Bob's wife, through his bedroom door, averring that he was deeply asleep through exhaustion. In the evening, when he felt better, Bob rang Rita and tried to ease her mind about the collapse in the park, about which she had now heard through the general grapevine.

The next scheduled tour date was on Tuesday night in Pittsburgh, and the Wailers and I-Threes travelled there on the Monday in readiness. Bob told Rita he would have to follow later, after some business matters in New York had been sorted. Dr Frazier didn't want him to tell anybody yet that he was actually going to see a specialist.

The New York neurologist did not take long to make his diagnosis, based on the evidence of X-ray photos and a brain scan. The collapse had indeed been a stroke, caused by a malignant brain tumour from which there was no hope of recovery. In fact, death could be within a matter of weeks, so advanced was the cancer. Bob, stunned, could scarcely believe what he was hearing. Dr Frazier, who was by contrast quite convinced, suggested that the tour should be cancelled forthwith, but Bob said he would go on to Pittsburgh anyway, possibly to see another doctor there.

Rita finally learned the truth when she phoned Bob's Pittsburgh hotel to discover why he was still not there. She too said the tour must be cancelled at once, but was told Bob wanted to carry on. Frightened and extremely angry, she warned the 'inner circle' that there would be major retributions if anything happened to Bob.

Bob arrived the next morning in the company of Alan Cole and Dr Frazier, looking scared, disorientated and not so much ill as ancient – he had begun to accept what he had been told by the doctors and it

Above: Rita Marley
Left: The Wailers without Bob

seemed that the realisation had added overnight the years he knew he would never experience. Most of those around him were urging him to play the night's show anyway, to keep going despite all: he would not listen to Rita's protests.

The concert went on, and Bob completed it, albeit in a somewhat truncated hour-and-a-half form (the rhythm section accelerated everything slightly to shorten each song's duration and conserve Bob's stamina), and minus much of his usual on-stage animation. Nevertheless, the audience were given no clue as to the gigantic significance of this night's show; the band even did five encores, including a solo acoustic version by Bob of his last major work Redemption Songs (recorded at the time, this version of the song would eventually be released in 1992 on the commemorative Songs Of Freedom 4-CD set). It was Bob Marley & the Wailers' last-ever public performance.

By Wednesday, the desperate Rita had marshalled her own troops, including Diane Jobson and Chris Blackwell, against those who were urging Bob to continue and wheels slammed into motion which stopped the tour immediately. The PR story went out that Bob had collapsed from exhaustion, and was in retreat to recuperate. Whisked back to Miami, he was sent for further tests at the Cedars of Lebanon Hospital, and then back to New York to be admitted to the Sloan-Kettering Cancer Center in Manhattan, where radiation therapy was started to try to check further growth of the brain tumour. Further tests, however, only made the news worse, as the Sloan-Kettering doctors detected additional cancers in Bob's lungs, liver and stomach. Word quickly leaked out to the media that Bob Marley was a patient at the hospital undergoing cancer treatment, and both the cover story and his incognito presence were blown. In an attempt to maintain at least his privacy, Bob moved out into first a hotel room and then to Danny Sims' New York home, while attending Sloan-Kettering daily as an outpatient. For a while, the radiation treatment rallied him, but after another stroke he lost the use of his legs and the doctors moved him on to chemotherapy, which caused his dreadlocks to fall out and his weight to plummet.

Now at last genuinely fearing for his life, so sick did he feel most of the time, Bob agreed with the regular requests by Rita and his mother that he be baptised into the Ethiopian Orthodox Church. The baptism took place on November 4, without anybody informing the Twelve Tribes of Israel (which held Bob as one of its own) of the decision. In a

Marley during his therapy at Dr Issels' cancer clinic in Rottach-Egern, Germany, which he attended with his mother and private doctor

service conducted at New York's Wellington hotel by the church's American head, Archbishop Yesuhaq, he received baptism as Berhane Selassie (Light of the Holy Trinity), in the presence of his distraught wife and children.

Knowing that Bob was not likely to outlast the year, Dr Frazier made what he considered the only worthwhile stab at seeking an alternative treatment. He contacted the West German specialist Dr Josef Issels, whose clinic in Bad Wiessee, beside Lake Tegernsee in the Bavarian Alps, had been treating officially hopeless cancer patients using unconventional methods in a 'holistic' approach that had virtually outlawed him from the international medical establishment for many years. Issels agreed to take Bob as a patient, and he was flown immediately to Germany via London, accompanied by Rita, Cedella, Dr Frazier, Alan Cole and Diane Jobson. The entourage arrived at Issels' clinic on November 9.

Despite the fact that Issels did not say that he could save Bob, merely help, a rapport developed between physician and patient which had Bob rallying, albeit in minor ways, on several occasions over the successive months in the Bavarian clinic. His treatment involved oxygenated blood transfusions, hyperthermia (ultraviolet heat) sessions, a tightly controlled diet, the injection of more than one anti-cancer drug banned in conventional medicine, and simple exercise in the open air. On this régime, living among a flexible group of those closest to him, in a rented flat only a few minutes' walk from the clinic, he survived the end of the year, his 36th birthday in February 1981 (when he was visited at the clinic by Wailers Tyrone Downie, Junior Marvin and Seeco Patterson), and into the spring. His whereabouts had been successfully kept secret for the first few weeks, with friends, family, Tuff Gong and Island Records all denying cancer stories and floating a red herring tale about Bob recuperating from extreme exhaustion in rural Ethiopia. By the end of 1980, however, the media had inevitably sniffed out the truth, and the world knew that Bob was in Germany and unlikely to live.

In March, Bob was interviewed at the clinic by a *Daily Mail* writer, and was clearly in positive spirits, pointing out to the reporter than it was possible to live past all the predictions, because he had already done it. So comparatively upbeat was the *Mail* story when it was published, that other media began to extrapolate rather too creatively, speculating that Bob would return to Jamaica by the middle of the year to resume his career. Return to Jamaica by that time he would indeed, but there was no more music to be made.

Bob continued to lose weight, and grew proportionally weaker, feeling at one stage unable to eat, drink or walk the few yards to the clinic. There came a time when he could no longer hold his guitar, and

eventually when he could not lift his Bible or concentrate to read it: Cedella or Diane Jobson read it to him instead. The crunch came on May 3, when Dr Issels confirmed that nothing more could be done, and that Bob's life was now likely to be measured in days. He suggested to Diane Jobson that she and the family might want to take Bob home while he still had strength enough to stand a plane flight. A private jet was chartered, and in a couple of days Bob, immobile but still comprehending, was back in Miami, to be rushed straight to Cedars of Lebanon hospital. Cedella, Rita and Diane expected nothing else when the doctor who admitted him said that his stay would not be long, but that the hospital could ease any final agony.

On Monday, May 11, only two days after reaching Miami, Bob finally died, in comparative peace, at around 11.40 am. Rita, Cedella and Diane were all present, and his last words were for his mother, asking her not to cry, because he would be all right.

As the news of Bob Marley's passing flashed across Jamaica and around the world, he was widely eulogised not only in the music media, but in print and on broadcast programmes of all kinds, transcending the fact that this, ostensibly, was merely the loss of an entertainer; when

Opposite: Thousands accompany the funeral cortège as it heads towards Bob's native village of Nine Miles
Right: Ziggy Marley in concert at the Beacon Theatre, New York

Bob died, a major cultural figure was removed from the 20th century landscape. Perhaps to its credit, the world at large recognised the fact, and praised his achievements accordingly.

Bob's body was laid out in a partially open coffin at his Miami home, three days after he died, and a memorial service was held in the house which was attended by many of his friends and acquaintances from far and wide, including Chris Blackwell, Danny Sims, and even the previously-estranged Don Taylor, along with past and present members of the Wailers.

Bob's body was flown home to Jamaica eight days after his death, in preparation for the State Funeral which the government of Edward Seaga (who had won the general election the previous October, in Bob's absence) had asked Rita Marley permission to give the man who was now regarded as a vital loss to the nation of his birth. Just one month before, the government had awarded Bob, again in absentia, the Jamaican Order of Merit – one of the highest honours at its disposal, and one which officially nominated him a national hero. Some questioned the integrity of such an award from a government formed by the political party which had been implicitly involved in the attempt to murder Marley in 1976. Others rejoiced that the prophet had finally found honour in his own country, even though he was slowly dying in a German clinic on the day that the Order of Merit was presented to his eldest son Ziggy on his behalf. Bob was now the Honorable Robert Nesta Marley, O.M. On Wednesday, May 20, Bob's body was laid in state in Kingston's national arena, giving more than 40,000 Jamaicans a chance to file past his coffin as though he were royalty. Clearly, for many of the tearful throng, he had been Jamaica's closest thing to it.

On Thursday 21, the day of the funeral itself, another memorial service was held at Kingston's main Ethiopian Orthodox Church, after which Bob's coffin was laid in a motorcade which drove – via Tuff Gong headquarters at Hope Road – back to the National Arena for the State Funeral at 11am. First the Wailers, then Cedella and her daughter Pearl, and finally Rita and the I-Threes, sang moving musical tributes, before Archbishop Yesuhaq, who only months previously had presided over Bob Marley's baptism, now took charge of his farewell. Lessons were read by Jamaica's Governor-General Florizel Glasspole, Michael Manley, and Bob's closest friend Alan Cole, before Edward Seaga provided a eulogy. Then, representatives from the Twelve Tribes of Israel carried

the coffin back to the motorcade, which slowly made the winding journey (followed by a positive carnival of other vehicles) north from the city to Bob's birthplace of Nine Miles, St. Ann. Along the 50-odd mile journey, the road was lined with people as, it seemed, the entire Jamaican population turned out to bid Bob Marley farewell. On arriving at its destination, a full five hours after setting out, the coffin was carried up the hill at the top of which stood the hut in which Bob had been born, and he was finally laid to rest there in a small concrete mausoleum which had been built adjacent to the house. As the Archbishop intoned the last rites, and Cedella and Rita sang a hymn, watched by the Prime Minister and more people than the St. Ann hills had ever previously seen together in one place, the tomb was systematically sealed and cemented shut. This action was more than merely symbolic, since Prophet Gad, leader of the Twelve Tribes of Israel, had been making increasing noises about wishing to have Bob Marley's ring, the relic of Haile Selassie, released into the keeping of his sect. In accordance with Bob's stated wish, and also his mother's ardent desire, the ring remained on Bob's finger after he died, and was still there in his coffin as it was finally interred, but nobody was willing to underestimate the desire of certain Twelve Tribes elements to obtain what they regarded as a holy relic. As evening fell and the huge mourning party slowly melted away from Nine Miles, however, the only Rastafarians present at the scene

Above: Ziggy Marley, carrying on in his father's footsteps
Left: Another member of the legacy, Bunny Wailer

had no interest in Haile Selassie's ring, but were those who chose to meditate and keep vigil over the tomb of Bob Marley.

In the years that followed his death, there was much to keep the name Bob Marley alive in the public consciousness – indeed, it remains a potent presence even more than a decade on from his passing.

Firstly, there was the question of the Marley inheritance. Bob had died apparently without leaving a will, which meant that the entire Tuff Gong organisation, plus Bob's ongoing earnings from record sales and songwriting royalties, reverted to Rita, on behalf of herself and Bob's eleven legal dependents, his children. After a while, a will turned up which demonstrated that this was what Bob had intended in any case. Slowly and methodically, Rita then remodelled the Tuff Gong empire (without Diane Jobson, who resigned when Bob died) in what might be described as her own image. 56 Hope Road became the Bob Marley Museum, which it remains today, one of Kingston's major draws for

After increasing involvement in the campaign to legal marijuana, Peter Tosh's life was to end tragically and violently

European and American tourists. The offices and recording studio were moved to a new complex on Marcus Garvey Drive, where Tuff Gong International also flourishes today as Jamaica's major internal record distributor, as well as still being the purveyor of Bob Marley's music to the world at large.

Rita has kept a firm hand on most things Marley-related to this day, but in 1987 the administration of the estate was suddenly wrenched from her hands by the Jamaican Supreme Court, following allegations that she had conspired with Bob's New York legal representatives David Steinberg and Marvin Zolt to conceal from the Jamaican Estate wide off-shore assets held by Bob, and there began to be suspicion about the authenticity of the 1978-dated Bob Marley will, too. In 1988, a year after Rita was forced to resign as administrator, the Jamaican government put Bob's estate, consisting of his recordings, his song catalogue and all the composer's rights relating to it, plus the houses and other real estate he had owned, up for sale. Although the Marley family contested it, this sale was eventually made, to Chris Blackwell's New York-based Island Logic Inc (the only serious bidder, as it happened) for $8.6 million – a large amount of money, but still a small sum, it might be thought, for assets with the continued income potential that the Bob Marley musical legacy clearly retained. Ironically, PolyGram, the multi-national record company which had been ready to sign Bob in a multi-million dollar deal just prior to his death, got his life's work anyway, in the end, somewhat by default: Chris Blackwell sold Island in its entirety to PolyGram in 1989, while retaining some creative control over the company he founded and had run for almost 30 years.

Rita Marley raised the profile of her own recording career in the years following Bob's death, while her fellow I-Threes, Judy Mowatt and Marcia Griffiths, both of whom had always prolifically recorded in their own right during the days when they sang with the Wailers, also continued their solo careers. Despite Jamaican hits, however, none of the women were to make a noticeable impact on the international market, and from that point of view, the chief inheritors of Bob Marley's global acclaim were his son Ziggy with the Melody Makers, the vocal group consisting of Bob and Rita's three eldest children and their adopted sister, Rita's daughter Sharon. The group had originally come together to cut Bob's song Children Playing In The Streets, released by Tuff Gong in Jamaica in 1979. Allegedly, they took their name from a copy of the UK

music weekly *Melody Maker* which pictured Bob on its front page. The group initially remained fairly low-key, despite Tuff Gong obtaining an international recording contract for them with EMI America. A breakthrough came, however, when they switched labels to Virgin in 1988, and recorded the album Conscious Party. This was a major success in America, selling over a million copies and making No.23 on the US chart – which was higher than all but a handful of their father's albums had managed. A hit single, Tomorrow People, was taken from the album, hitting No.39 in the US and No.22 in the UK.

Two more successful albums by Ziggy and the group – One Bright Day in 1989 and Jahmekya in 1991 – kept their profile high and ensured touring success on a par (in terms of audience size and box office receipts) with that of Bob & the Wailers a decade earlier. The mid-90s are proving a quieter period, but there is little doubt that Bob Marley's oldest son and his siblings still have more music to offer the world yet.

The Wailers, in a true sense, disbanded as soon as Bob had played his last concert. Antipathy grew between the various musicians and the Marley estate over royalties from the recordings they had made with Bob, and eventually a take-it-or-leave-it contract was offered to each individual by which they gave up all future claims and rights in return

for a one-off cash payment. None chose to leave it; the pressure being applied to ease Bob's former band out of more than a historical share in his legacy was too great. Most of them moved elsewhere in the Jamaican musical community, or to the US, and none was to come to particular prominence in any future musical development. Various members would, however, regroup for Bob Marley tributes, birthday concerts, and so on, and eventually a touring group called the Wailers Band emerged, based mainly around Junior Marvin and Family Man Barrett, occasionally joined by others of their former stellar fraternity. Notable and regrettably permanent absentee is Family Man's brother Carlton, the Wailers' long-time anchorman at the drums. He was shot dead at his home on April 17, 1987, in a domestic slaying apparently engineered by his wife Albertimne and her lover.

Bunny Livingston, under his preferred performer's name of Bunny Wailer, has continued to make music until the present day. His path fol-

The headquarters of Tuff Gong Records, decorated with Marley record sleeves and photographs, in Kingston, Jamaica

lowing the original Wailers' split was always one well divergent from Bob's, and his music tended to be more personally orientated – whether it was deeply spiritual or unashamedly dancefloor-aimed (and Bunny has always swung freely between the two and several points in between). What has continued to escape him, though, has been international commercial success – he has never had a hit single or album in either America or the UK.

Peter Tosh's story, however, was another that finally ran to tragedy. Always closer to Bob after the original Wailers split, and not unknown sharing a stage with his former partner, Peter's solo music – which was invariably Rasta-political and frequently heavy in marijuana legalisation propaganda – did find wider international acclaim. Six of his albums made the US chart, though mostly in moderate fashion (the highest-placed reached No.59), between 1976's Legalise It and 1984's Captured Live. His association with Mick Jagger and subsequent signing to the Rolling Stones label towards the end of the 1970s even gave him a transatlantic hit single, (You Got To Walk And) Don't Look Back, duetted with Jagger and taken from the Bush Doctor album, which made No.43 in the UK and No.81 in the US chart.

However, only five months after the murder of Carlie Barrett, Tosh too was shot dead at his home on September 11, 1987, when he was 42 years old. His killer was a former acquaintance named Dennis Lobban, who apparently held a long-term grudge. Shortly after being released from prison, Lobban attempted to rob Tosh's house while holding up Peter, his wife and two guests with a gun. Somewhere along the way, somebody panicked, Lobban freaked and shot all his hostages – two of them, including Peter Tosh, fatally. Lobban was arrested for murder and sentenced to hanging.

Bob's own music has continued, posthumously, to enthral the world in the decade or more since his passing. As the Marley legend continued to grow, interest was such that when archive material from Tuff Gong's and Island's vaults was released – in gratifyingly sparing quantities – for public consumption, an avid market was there to eagerly snap it up. In the UK, for instance, Bob Marley had several of his biggest commercial successes after he died.

The first posthumous release was a less than welcome one, when, late in 1981, Danny Sims put out a compilation entitled Chances Are through the Atlantic Records subsidiary Cotillion. This was comprised of various songs which Bob had recorded, some of them as demos, during his late-60s songwriting stint for Cayman Music, as well as the tracks (including the single Reggae On Broadway) cut for CBS shortly before the Wailers signed to Island. Critics pounced upon the album with scarcely-controlled wrath, widely viewing it as little more than a cynical cash-in on the record sales inevitably generated by Bob's then-recent death. Any merits the formative material may have had in its own right were obscured by the crass circumstances of the release.

In May 1983, Island released Confrontation, a compilation of rare tracks, Jamaica-only singles, and several items which had been left uncompleted by Bob at the onset of his illness. Family Man Barrett and

other Wailers members completed the necessary instrumental overdubbing on these latter tracks before release. This album, which seemed true to the spirit of Bob's later work, was well received by the Marley audience, particularly in the UK, where it reached No.5 in the chart and where the extracted single Buffalo Soldier (recorded in 1978 in Miami with producer King Sporty) made No.4 – Bob's highest UK singles chart position ever. In the USA, Confrontation climbed to No.55 but, as usual, there was no American hit single.

In 1984 came Legend, a straightforward compilation of Bob's most celebrated songs, reaching from Stir It Up to Redemption Songs and including all the UK hit singles. This package was an incredible success, and has never stopped selling up to the present day: finally, here was the Bob Marley album for people who had never previously got around to buying Bob Marley albums, and literally millions of them went for it, to make it by far the biggest-selling Bob Marley record of all time. In the UK it topped the album chart for 12 consecutive weeks, spending an incredible total of 106 weeks in all in the top 75. British sales in the mid-1990s stand at around one-and-a-half million, and the compilation was

Damian Marley, Bob's son by his relationship with the former Miss Jamaica and Miss World, Cindy Breakspeare

Above: A makeshift shrine is assembled in commemoration of the 10th Anniversary of Marley's death
Left: Bob Marley Boulevard in Kingston; Opposite: (l to r) Cedella Marley, Cedella Booker-Marley, Rita Marley in 1994

the 32nd best-selling album of the 1980s in the UK. While it was topping the chart in 1984, the One Love/People Get Ready medley was taken from the LP as a single, and made No.5. In the US, the album had a more modest peak chart position (No.54), but also continued to sell consistently and healthily for years afterwards – its current US sales are over three million.

In later years, two further albums appeared, with less obvious commercial potential, but of great interest to followers of Bob's music. Rebel Music, in mid-1986, offered mostly familiar songs in not-so-familiar versions, while 1991's Talking Blues consisted mainly of rare performances taken from a radio broadcast on KSAN, San Francisco, recorded during the Wailers' 1973 tour, and also included Bob's spoken thoughts on his life and music.

Bob Lives!
Bob Marley's mother, Cedella Booker-Marley, outside the house where he was born in 1945, in the northern Jamaican village of Nine Miles.

The most comprehensive look at Bob Marley's musical legacy came in 1992 with the compilation Songs Of Freedom. Taking advantage of the huge growth in popularity of the CD boxed retrospective market, this was a handsomely conceived set combining a high-quality hardback book with four compact discs, containing in all 77 tracks which told the entire Marley musical story from Judge Not, the first-ever recording, through to the solo version of Redemption Song taped at his last-ever concert in Pittsburgh. Diligent work by the compilers also found a wealth of never-released material, a lot of which was also included on the set, such as an acoustic medley of early songs taped by John Bundrick during Bob's 1971 film soundtrack sojourn in Sweden.

One of the never-heard songs, Iron Lion Zion, became a No.5 hit single in the UK. Songs Of Freedom was acclaimed as one of the best reissue projects of 1992, and for an expensive boxed set, its sales of over a million have justified the painstaking work and attention to detail which went into its creation.

In January 1994, many years after his passing, another major honour was bestowed upon Bob Marley, when he was inducted in Philadelphia, USA, into the Rock and Roll Hall of Fame – an élite honour bestowed only on artists whose music can be said to have had both a major impact and a clear influence on the rock field as a whole over a long period. The company in the hall of fame is truly stellar: Elvis Presley, the Beatles, Chuck Berry, the Rolling Stones, James Brown and other such international superstars whose music has never faded and still makes a vibrant contribution to popular culture. So much can also be said for Bob Marley, the first Third World artist to stand in their ranks, and still casting his musical spell around the globe.

SELECTIVE DISCOGRAPHY

The Island/Tuff Gong Albums

CATCH A FIRE (Island ILPS 9241)
Tracks: Concrete Jungle / Slave Driver / 400 Years / Stop That Train /
Rock It Baby (Baby We've Got A Date) / Stir It Up / Kinky Reggae /
No More Trouble / Midnight Ravers
Produced: Bob Marley & Chris Blackwell
Released: April 1973

BURNIN' (Island ILPS 9256)
Tracks: Get Up, Stand Up / Hallelujah Time / I Shot The Sheriff /
Burnin' And Lootin' / Put It On / Small Axe / Pass It On / Duppy
Conqueror / One Foundation / Rastaman Chant
Produced: Bob Marley & Chris Blackwell
Released: November 1973

NATTY DREAD (Island ILPS 9281)
Tracks: Lively Up Yourself / No Woman, No Cry / Them Belly Full
(But We Hungry) / Rebel Music (3 O'Clock Road Block) / So Jah Seh /
Natty Dread / Bend Down Low / Talkin' Blues / Revolution
Produced: The Wailers & Chris Blackwell
Released: January 1975

LIVE! (Island ILPS 9376)
Tracks: Trench Town Rock / Burnin' And Lootin' / Them Belly Full
(But We Hungry) / Lively Up Yourself / No Woman, No Cry / I Shot
The Sheriff / Get Up, Stand Up
Produced: Steve Smith & Chris Blackwell
Released: November 1975

RASTAMAN VIBRATION (Island ILPS 9383)
Tracks: Positive Vibration / Roots, Rock, Reggae / Johnny Was / Cry
To Me / Want More / Crazy Baldhead / Who The Cap Fit / Night
Shift / War / Rat Race
Produced: Bob Marley & the Wailers
Released: April 1976

EXODUS (Island ILPS 9498)
Tracks: Natural Mystic / So Much Things To Say / Guiltiness / The
Heathen / Exodus / Jammin' / Waiting In Vain / Turn Your Lights
Down Low / Three Little Birds / One Love - People Get Ready
Produced: Bob Marley & The Wailers
Released: May 1977

KAYA (Island ILPS 9517)
Tracks: Easy Skanking /
Kaya / Sun Is Shining / Is
This Love? / Satisfy My Soul
/ She's Gone / Misty
Morning / Crisis / Running
Away / Time Will Tell
*Produced: Bob Marley &
the Wailers*
Released: March 1978

BABYLON BY BUS (Island
ILDS 11 - double album)
Tracks: Positive Vibration /
Punky Reggae Party /
Exodus / Stir It Up / Rat
Race / Concrete Jungle /
Kinky Reggae / Lively Up
Yourself / Rebel Music /
War / No More Trouble / Is
This Love? / Heathen /
Jammin'

Produced: Bob Marley & the Wailers
Released: November 1978

SURVIVAL (Island ILPS 9542)
Tracks: So Much Trouble In The World / Zimbabwe / Top Rankin' /
Babylon System / Survival / Africa Unite / One Drop / Ride Natty
Ride / Ambush In The Night / Wake Up And Live
Produced: Bob Marley & the Wailers & Alex Sadkin
Released: October 1979

UPRISING (Island ILPS 9596)
Tracks: Coming In From The Cold / Real Situation / Bad Card / We
And Dem / Work / Zion Train / Pimper's Paradise / Could You Be
Loved / Forever Loving Jah / Redemption Song
Produced: Bob Marley & the Wailers
Released: June 1980

CONFRONTATION (Island ILPS 9760)
Tracks: Chant Down Babylon / Buffalo Soldier / Jump Niyahbinghi /
Mix Up, Mix Up / Give Thanks And Praises / Blackman Redemption /
Trench Town / Stiff Neck Fools / I Know / Rastaman Live Up
Produced: The Wailers & Chris Blackwell
Released: May 1983

LEGEND (Island BMW 1)
Tracks: Is This Love? / No Woman, No Cry / Could You Be Loved /
Three Little Birds / Buffalo Soldier / Get Up, Stand Up / Stir It Up /
One Love - People Get Ready / I Shot The Sheriff / Waiting In Vain /
Redemption Song / Satisfy My Soul / Exodus / Jammin'
Produced: Various (compilation)
Released: May 1984

REBEL MUSIC (Island
ILPS 9843)
Tracks: Rebel Music /
So Much Trouble In
The World / Them
Belly Full (But We
Hungry) / Rat Race /
War - No More
Trouble / Roots / Slave
Driver / Ride, Natty,
Ride / Crazy Baldhead /
Get Up, Stand Up
*Produced: Various
(compilation)*
Released: July 1986

TALKIN' BLUES (Tuff Gong TGLLP 12)
Tracks: Talkin' Blues / Burnin' And Lootin' / Kinky Reggae / Get Up,
Stand Up / Slave Driver / Walk The Proud Land / You Can't Blame
The Youth / Rastaman Chant / Am-A-Do / Bend Down Low / I Shot
The Sheriff
Produced: KSAN Radio Production
Released: March 1991

SONGS OF FREEDOM (Tuff Gong TGCBX 1 - 4-CD set)
Tracks: Judge Not / One Cup Of Coffee / Simmer Down / I'm Still
Waiting / One Love - People Get Ready / Put It On / Bus Dem Shut
(Pyaka) / Mellow Mood / Bend Down Low / Hypocrites / Stir It Up /
Nice Time / Thank You Lord / Hammer / Caution / Back Out / Soul
Shakedown Party / Do It Twice / Soul Rebel / Sun Is Shining / Don't
Rock The Boat / Small Axe / Duppy Conqueror / Mr Brown / Screw
Face / Lick Samba / Trench Town Rock / Craven Choke Puppy /
Guava Jelly / Acoustic Medley: Guava Jelly - This Train -
Cornerstone - Comma Comma - Dewdrops - Stir It Up - I'm Hurting
Inside / I'm Hurting Inside / High Tide Or Low Tide / Slave Driver /
No More Trouble / Concrete Jungle / Get Up, Stand Up / Rastaman
Chant / Burnin' And Lootin' / Iron Lion Zion / Lively Up Yourself /
Natty Dread / I Shot The Sheriff / No Woman, No Cry / Who The
Cap Fit / Jah Live / Crazy Baldheads / War / Johnny Was / Rat Race /
Jammin' / Waiting In Vain / Exodus / Natural Mystic / Three Little
Birds / Running Away / Keep On Moving / Easy Skanking / Is This
Love? / Smile Jamaica / Time Will Tell / Africa Unite / Survival / One
Drop / One Dub / Zimbabwe / So Much Trouble In The World /

Ride Nay Ride / Babylon System / Coming In From The Cold / Real
Situation / Bad Card / Could You Be Loved / Forever Loving Jah /
Rastaman Live Up / Give Thanks And Praise / One Love - People
Get Ready / Why Should I / Redemption Song
*Produced: Various (compilation) Compiled by Trevor Wyatt &
Neville Garrick*
Released: September 1992
NB: All Island/Tuff Gong albums have subsequently been released
on CD, with different catalogue numbers.

Non-Island Collections

THE VERY BEST OF THE EARLY YEARS (Music Club MCCD 033)
Tracks: Trench Town Rock* / Lively Up Yourself * / Soul Almighty /
Wisdom / Caution / Cheer Up / Thank You Lord / Stop The Train /
This Time / Small Axe / More Axe / Don't Rock My Boat / Keep On
Moving / Brand New Second Hand / Kaya / Turn Me Loose / Sun Is
Shining / Keep On Skanking
*Produced: Clement Dodd /Lee Perry/*Bob Marley*
Released: September 1991

THE LEE PERRY SESSIONS (Charly CPCD 8009 - CD compilation)
Tracks: Lively Up Yourself / Small Axe / Trench Town Rock / Sun Is
Shining / Kaya / African Herbsman / Brain Washing / Mr Brown /
Try Me / No Sympathy / Duppy Conqueror / Stand Alone / Fussing
And Fighting / Rebel's Hop / Soul Almighty / It's Alright / Don't
Rock The Boat / Put It On / All In One / Keep On Moving
Produced: Lee Perry
Released: October 1993